Satire

Forms of Drama

Forms of Drama meets the need for accessible, mid-length volumes that offer undergraduate readers authoritative guides to the distinct forms of global drama. From classical Greek tragedy to Chinese pear garden theatre, cabaret to *kathakali*, the series equips readers with models and methodologies for analysing a wide range of performance practices and engaging with these as 'craft'.

SERIES EDITOR: SIMON SHEPHERD

Cabaret
978-1-3501-4025-7
William Grange

Pageant
978-1-3501-4451-4
Joan FitzPatrick Dean

Satire
978-1-3501-4007-3
Joel Schechter

Tragicomedy
978-1-3501-4430-9
Brean Hammond

Satire

Joel Schechter

methuen | drama

LONDON • NEW YORK • OXFORD • NEW DELHI • SYDNEY

METHUEN DRAMA
Bloomsbury Publishing Plc
50 Bedford Square, London, WC1B 3DP, UK
1385 Broadway, New York, NY 10018, USA
29 Earlsfort Terrace, Dublin 2, Ireland

BLOOMSBURY, METHUEN DRAMA and the Methuen Drama logo are
trademarks of Bloomsbury Publishing Plc

First published in Great Britain 2021

A catalogue record for this book is available from the British Library.

Library of Congress Control Number: 2021938157

ISBN: HB: 978-1-3501-4008-0
          PB: 978-1-3501-4007-3
          ePDF: 978-1-3501-4010-3
          eBook: 978-1-3501-4009-7

Series: Forms of Drama

Typeset by Integra Software Services Pvt. Ltd.

To find out more about our authors and books visit www.bloomsbury.com
and sign up for our newsletters.

CONTENTS

LIST OF
ILLUSTRATIONS

SERIES PREFACE

The scope of this series is scripted aesthetic activity that works by means of personation.

Scripting is done in a wide variety of ways. It may, most obviously, be the more or less detailed written text familiar in the stage play of the Western tradition, which not only provides lines to be spoken but directions for speaking them. Or it may be a set of instructions, a structure or scenario, on the basis of which performers improvise, drawing, as they do so, on an already learnt repertoire of routines and responses. Or there may be nothing written, just sets of rules, arrangements, and even speeches orally handed down over time. The effectiveness of such unwritten scripting can be seen in the behaviour of audiences, who, without reading a script, have learnt how to conduct themselves appropriately at the different activities they attend. For one of the key things that unwritten script specifies and assumes is the relationship between the various groups of participants, including the separation, or not, between doers and watchers.

What is scripted is specifically an aesthetic activity. That specification distinguishes drama from non-aesthetic activity using personation. Following the work of Erving Goffman in the mid-1950s, especially his book *The Presentation of Self in Everyday Life*, the social sciences have made us richly aware of the various ways in which human interactions are performed. Going shopping, for example, is a performance in that we present a version of ourselves in each encounter we make. We may indeed have changed our clothes before setting out. This, though, is a social performance.

The distinction between social performance and aesthetic activity is not clear-cut. The two sorts of practice overlap and mingle with one another. An activity may be more or less aesthetic, but the crucial distinguishing feature is the status of the aesthetic element. Going shopping may contain an aesthetic element – decisions about clothes and shoes to wear – but its purpose is not deliberately to make an aesthetic activity or to mark itself as different from everyday social life. The aesthetic element is not regarded as a general requirement. By contrast a court-room trial may be seen as a social performance, in that it has an important social function, but it is at the same time extensively scripted, with prepared speeches, costumes, and choreography. This scripted aesthetic element assists the social function in that it conveys a sense of more than everyday importance and authority to proceedings which can have lifechanging impact. Unlike the activity of going shopping the aesthetic element here is not optional. Derived from tradition it is a required component that gives the specific identity to the activity.

It is defined as an activity in that, in a way different from a painting of Rembrandt's mother or a statue of Ramesses II, something is made to happen over time. And, unlike a symphony concert or firework display, that activity works by means of personation. Such personation may be done by imitating and interpreting – 'inhabiting' – other human beings, fictional or historical, and it may use the bodies of human performers or puppets. But it may also be done by a performer who produces a version of their own self, such as a stand-up comedian or court official on duty, or by a performer who, through doing the event, acquires a self with special status as with the *hijras* securing their sacredness by doing the ritual practice of *badhai*.

Some people prefer to call many of these sorts of scripted aesthetic events not drama but cultural performance. But there are problems with this. First, such labelling tends to keep in place an old-fashioned idea of Western scholarship that drama, with its origins in ancient Greece, is a specifically European 'high' art. Everything outside it is then potentially, and damagingly, consigned to a domain which may be neither 'art' nor 'high'. Instead the European stage play and its like can best be regarded as a subset of the general category, distinct from the rest in that two groups of people come together in order specifically to present and watch a story being acted out by imitating other persons and settings. Thus, the performance of a stage play in this tradition consists of two levels of activity using personation: the interaction of audience and performers and the interaction between characters in a fictional story.

The second problem with the category of cultural performance is that it downplays the significance and persistence of script, in all its varieties. With its roots in the traditional behaviours and beliefs of a society script gives specific instructions for the form – the materials, the structure, and sequence – of the aesthetic activity, the drama. So too, as we have noted, script defines the relationships between those who are present in different capacities at the event.

It is only by attending to what is scripted, to the form of the drama, that we can best analyse its functions and pleasures. At its most simple analysis of form enables us to distinguish between different sorts of aesthetic activity. The masks used in *kathakali* look different from those used in *commedia dell'arte*. They are made of different materials, designs, and colours. The roots of those differences lie in their separate cultural traditions and systems of living. For similar reasons the puppets of *karagoz* and *wayang* differ. But perhaps more importantly the attention to form provides a basis for exploring the operation and effects of a particular work. Those who regularly participate in and watch drama, of whatever sort, learn to recognize and remember the forms of what they see and hear. When one drama has family resemblances to another, in its organization and use of materials, structure, and sequences, those who attend it develop expectations as to how it will – or indeed should – operate. It then becomes possible to specify how a particular work subverts, challenges, or enhances these expectations.

Expectation doesn't only govern response to individual works, however. It can shape, indeed has shaped, assumptions about which dramas are worth studying. It is well established that Asia has ancient and rich dramatic traditions, from the Indian sub-continent to Japan, as does Europe, and these are studied with enthusiasm. But there is much less widespread activity, at least in Western universities, in relation to the traditions of, say, Africa, Latin America, and the Middle East. Second, even within the recognized traditions, there are assumptions that some dramas are more 'artistic', or indeed more 'serious', 'higher' even, than others. Thus, it may be assumed that *noh* or classical tragedy will require the sort of close attention to craft which is not necessary for mumming or *badhai*.

Both sets of assumptions here keep in place a system which allocates value. This series aims to counteract a discriminatory value system by ranging as widely as possible across world practices and by giving the same sort of attention to all the forms it features. Thus book-length studies of forms such as *al-halqa, hana keaka and ta'zieh* will appear in English for perhaps the first time. Those studies, just like those of kathakali, tragicomedy, and the rest, will adopt the same basic approach. That approach consists of an historical overview of the development of a form combined with, indeed anchored in, detailed analysis of examples and case studies. One of the benefits of properly detailed analysis is that it can reveal the construction which gives a work the appearance of being serious, artistic, and indeed 'high'. What does that work of construction is script. This series is grounded in the idea that all forms of drama have script of some kind and that an understanding of drama, of any sort, has to include analysis of that script. In taking this approach, books in this series again challenge an assumption which has in recent times governed the study of drama. Deriving from the supposed, but artificial, distinction between cultural performance and drama, many accounts of cultural performance ignore its scriptedness and assume that the proper way of studying it is simply to describe how its practitioners behave and what they make. This is useful enough, but to leave it at that is to produce something that looks like a form of lesser anthropology. The description of behaviours is only the first step in that it establishes what the script is. The next step is to analyse how the script and form work and how they create effect.

But it goes further than this. The close-up analyses of materials, structures, and sequences – of scripted forms – show how they emerge from and connect deeply back into the modes of life and belief to which they are necessary. They tell us in short why, in any culture, the drama needs to be done. Thus by adopting the extended model of drama, and by approaching all dramas in the same way, the books in this series aim to tell us why, in all societies, the activities of scripted aesthetic personation – dramas – keep happening, and need to keep happening.

I am grateful, as always, to Mick Wallis for helping me to think through these issues. Any clumsiness or stupidity is entirely my own.

Simon Shepherd

ACKNOWLEDGEMENTS

I want to thank friends and colleagues for their help during the writing of this volume. I received considerable encouragement and advice from Ron Jenkins, Joan Holden, Diana Scott, R.G. Davis, Peter Thomson, Lawrence Eilenberg, Sukanya Chakrabarti, Geoff Hoyle, Lawrence Bush, Florentina Mocanu-Schendel, Eric Schechter and Marc Silberman. I also remain grateful to the editor of this book's series, Simon Shepherd, project manager Suriya Rajasekar, and Lara Bateman and Mark Dudgeon at Methuen Drama. Illustrations are used through arrangement with Getty Images.

Joel Schechter

ACKNOWLEDGEMENTS

1

Introduction: What Was Stage Satire? Looking Back at an Endangered Art Form

Stage satire has been applauded for thousands of years; but the applause for this form of theatre erupts less often today than in the past when Aristophanes, John Gay and other playwrights prompted audiences to laugh volubly at scenes of misconduct. They ridiculed prominent individuals and institutions of their day in plays that merit the kind of praise Jonathan Swift gave *The Beggar's Opera* after it opened in 1728. John Gay's satire, said Swift, excels in humour that 'laughs Men out of their Follies and Vices' (1730: 21). He thought the play would probably do more good than a thousand sermons. Three centuries later, as we approach the tercentenary of *The Beggar's Opera*, the amount of folly and vice in the world has not diminished, sermons are still heard on Sundays and the efficacy Swift attributed to stage satire has been considerably reduced, along with the audience for it.

Before its decline in popularity, satiric theatre attracted sizable audiences. In London, John Gay's satire ran for sixty-two nights in its first season, setting attendance records and making its producer wealthy. *The Beggar's Opera* became the talk of the town and encouraged imitations of its form by other playwrights. In ancient Athens, 15,000 to 17,000 spectators sat together to see the single performance of a satire by Aristophanes. Greek festivals showed his new plays only one day a year; but year after year, thousands of Athenians watched plays by Aristophanes ridicule Greek legislators, philosophers, military generals, rival poets, husbands and wives, despite objections raised by a prominent general or two. The reprisals Aristophanes suffered for his satire did not deter him. One powerful opponent took the author to court; the satirist joked about the lawsuit in a subsequent play, and continued to win prizes in festival competitions.

Plays with the timeliness, wit and popularity of Aristophanes or John Gay are now an endangered species, as electronic media give live stage performances competition. Prospective audiences stay at home, or in front of a screen, instead of assembling in a theatre space in large numbers, as they did in earlier centuries to welcome the satires of Jonson, Molière, Fielding, Gogol, Meyerhold, Mayakovsky, Brecht, Soyinka, Behan, Fo and Littlewood, as well as Aristophanes and Gay. The considerable contributions of these artists still can be seen in revivals of the plays they created; but stage presentations of their calibre and audiences eager to watch their offerings are encountered more often today in documents of theatre history than in live performance.

Written for live performance, theatrical satire requires actors and audience to be present in a shared space and acknowledge one another for the artistry to be fully realized. It is a participatory art, with scenes staged for spectator responses, particularly laughter and assent to a play's mockery of well-known individuals. Stripped of scenery, lighting, comic actors and audience after a performance ends, accomplishments of this ephemeral form are harder to assess than satiric novels, poems or mock-travelogues such as *Gulliver's Travels* which can be read (and need not be heard) at any time. Texts that offer satire without actors get most of the attention from critics of the art. M.H. Abrams, for example, defines 'satire' as 'the literary art of diminishing or derogating a subject by making it ridiculous and evoking toward it attitudes of amusement, contempt, scorn or indignation... Comedy evokes laughter mainly as an end in itself, while satire "derides"; that is, it uses laughter as a weapon' (1985: 187). Abrams's references to derogation, weaponized laughter and ridicule are fine; he even tacitly admits the need for a respondent in his reference to laughter. But the thought that satire can be more than a 'literary art' and take shape on stage appears only briefly toward the end of his three-page gloss. To allow the form its due as theatre, a critic would have to consider the contributions of actors and directors abetted by designers, stagehands, financial backers, musicians and spectators, all of whom contribute to a performance that 'laughs Men out of their Follies and Vices'.

Even in literary satires such as *Gulliver's Travels*, though no actors are needed to read the book, different voices speak. Some readers and critics mistake the voice of Lemuel Gulliver or the projector in Swift's pamphlet *A Modest Proposal* for that of the satirist himself; but there is a distance between the author and his creations comparable to that between a playwright and stage characters. That distance gives the author license to write and actor license to speak things more outrageous than he or she would say in other circumstances.

When the playwright derogates or diminishes a subject on stage, it is done not only with words: also with exaggeration and distortion of facial expressions, physical movement, an ensemble of voices singing, debating, laughing. The alternately wry, dry, milquetoast and savage intonations with which an actor can deliver lines and various unruly and restrained gestures enhance whatever text is spoken. An author's voice may be detected somewhere in a play. But it also could elude spectators, as many voices are heard, many characters seen, many offenses offered and some taken.

In topical stage satire addressing contemporary issues, actors also engage in impersonation and embody the voices and physical behaviour of individuals widely known outside the theatre. When Aristophanes's text required mimicry of the tyrant Cleon in *The Knights*, the satire focused on an immensely powerful Athenian leader who sat, alive and in person, in the front row at the play's first and only performance in 424 BCE. No modern production of the play can reproduce those conditions; the Athenian audience, a specific leader and actors who mock that leader together in the present tense of performance made such satire on stage markedly different from other forms of expression. To appreciate *The Knights* today the play's original social, artistic and political contexts – the seating capacity of the theatre, the audience's backgrounds, the tyrant under attack – need to be known, and will be considered in pages that follow.

Satire on stage shares some characteristics with printed and electronic recordings of the art. Persons subjected to ridicule in any of these media are said to have questionable attributes; they exercise not just power but an excess of power, or they show arrogance, greed, hypocrisy, cowardice, self-love, other faults that lend themselves to caricature by an artist who distorts or exaggerates the behaviour for comic effect. To say that a satiric play attacks hypocrisy or greed would be insufficient; it finds these flaws in human behaviour, gives them faces, names, embodies them on stage with actors, holds them to account in a specific time and place, and it is not finished until an audience welcomes the result – or finds itself offended.

This Is What Democracy Looked Like

The art that ridicules immoderate behaviour occasionally has unreasonable limits and definitions imposed on it by critics. Kenneth MacLeish, in an introduction to Aristophanes, separates satiric art from political action when he quotes Philip Roth (satirist of American President Nixon in the novel *Our Gang*): 'Writing satire is a literary, not a political act, however volcanic the reformist or even revolutionary passion in the author. Satire is moral rage transformed into comic art' (Aristophanes 1993: xxvi). Certainly for Roth, who wrote novels and not plays, satire was a literary act, and he excelled at it; but performance of a play such as *The Knights* can be viewed as a political act, and a democratic act as it criticizes a tyrant in front of thousands of other Athenians. Performance of that play or one by Henry Fielding or Dario Fo ridiculing powerful men differs from conventional political action. It is not a protest march or a senatorial caucus; but *The Knights* and other satires performed for a public assembly are not entirely different from the texts delivered by legislators. Though legislatures may be less humorous, their speakers, like actors in satire, debate issues, initiate controversies, threaten opponents and may even come to blows.

Votes have played a role in both arenas too. In ancient Athens, ten of the spectators – drama festival contest judges – cast ballots to determine who won the competition among playwrights. Far more Athenian voters participated in decision-making outside the theatre. Many of those other Athenian voters watched satires in the Theatre of Dionysus. Only 6,000 citizens composed the governing Assembly in Athens, but the theatre accommodated up to 17,000. Actors and writers may not have had the authority of government officials; but they brought together a larger number of citizens than the Assembly, and their dialogues aired current issues at the same time they entertained spectators. In his book *Anatomy of Satire*, Gilbert Highet notes that portrayal of a political leader is liable to transgress the boundaries between satire and politics. The effort may begin as 'satiric parody' and 'pass out of the arts and into action' (1962: 92–3).

The issues Aristophanes aired were quite varied; not all of the plays focused on politicians. Positions held by wives and slaves, poets and philosophers, as well as assemblymen and generals were questioned with irreverence by the Athenian playwright, his actors and their chorus of twenty-four. A wide range of topics can be found in his stage satires and those that followed.

While Aristophanes, John Gay and Brendan Behan, three innovative writers, and their plays receive most of the attention in these pages, a few words need to be said in praise of another group contributing to their success: namely, past audiences. Since the advent of mass media, most prospective audiences for performance favour film, television and computer screenings over live theatre. The change enlarges viewership, but it also deprives satire of a live audience whose presence was important enough to be acknowledged in *The Knights*, in John Gay's *The Beggar's Opera* (1728) and Brendan Behan's *The Hostage* (1958), all three of which will be considered in more detail. 'All this we must do, to comply with the Taste of the Town,' claims a character named Player about his choices in Gay's stage satire (Gay 2013: 69). *The Beggar's Opera* actually changed the taste of the town, but first mocked its fashions, including the vogue of Italian opera. In *The Knights*, a slave ready to rebel promises 'upstanding citizens, and every smart spectator' 'will rally' to his side (Aristophanes 1998: 259). Here and in other cases, audience response to the satire was led by the playwright and performers. Objections the plays raised to faulty behaviour influenced behaviour, generated applause and a demand for tickets, and gave the satires by Gay and Behan long runs. While *The Knights* was scheduled for only one performance at its inception, its controversy continued after the festival ended. (Aristophanes settled the lawsuit out of court.) By contrast, televised screenings of a satiric performance may be rebroadcast occasionally; but an electronic version will not bring together an audience of thousands to laugh in like-minded company and marvel at its own numbers as well as the playwright's temerity.

During the pandemic of 2020, when theatres were closed to prevent the spread of illness, a *New York Times* critic lamented having to watch stage performances at home on her computer screen, 'experiencing them through a filter of a medium they weren't constructed for... they felt flattened and far away... relics of theater rather than theater itself' (Collins-Hughes 2020: C6). Even in a theatre seating 17,000 Athenians, those in the back rows could experience a sense of closeness, not only because the place was crowded; the actors shared scandals and accusations with them while a national leader and other prominent citizens subjected to the satire sat there. Audiences attending *The Knights*, *The Beggar's Opera* and *The Hostage* when those plays first opened would have been able to see in their midst some of the leaders satirized; witnessing a prominent leader confronted by comic critics, or watching a very important person's imitator mock him or her on stage, spectators could enjoy a kind of complicity and presence that camera close-ups cannot provide. Looking at theatrical satires by Aristophanes, Gay, Behan and a few others, we can begin to understand the kind of stage performances and audiences for them that are missing in our time.

The humorous invective, songs and jests these plays direct at demagogues, cheats, kidnappers, infatuated ingénues and high society fashion-plates do not necessarily improve with age. When first performed, popular stage satires thrive on references to people and events known to the public. A twenty-first-century audience will have difficulty gauging Cleon's importance to Athens 2,450 years after *The Knights* opened. Aristophanes's debunking of his city-state's tyrant is not likely to provoke audience laughter or win first prize as it did originally, although the play may evoke thoughts about other, more recent tyrants.

Satires that look at other sources of lying, greed and hypocrisy besides politicians often contain references that still resonate centuries after their first performance. The ridicule Gay, Behan and Aristophanes directed at the institution of marriage, for example, may be readily understood by contemporary spectators, although representations of relationships between men and women – and of same-sex relationships – have changed over time too. Only male actors performed women's roles in ancient Greek and Elizabethan drama; once actresses appeared in plays, satire of gender roles and matrimony was no longer fully controlled by men. Women's voices were heard, even if men wrote their lines. In *The Beggar's Opera*, when Jeremiah Peachum asks his newly married daughter Polly how she proposes to live, she answers, 'Like other Women, sir, upon the Industry of my Husband' (2013: 19). But her comic answer takes on additional meaning once we know that Lavinia Fenton, the actress who first portrayed Polly Peachum, earned her own living on stage. She needed no financial support from a husband. Polly Peachum's reply to her father retains some humour in any case, because the 'industry' of her spouse Macheath involves robbery, assault and gambling; she could not live 'like other Women' unless they too were married to notorious criminals.

Satire of this order remains humorous for centuries, but problems of humour with an expiration date and ephemeral topicality arise even in the best of plays. Remedies to the threat of obsolescence have been found in rewriting, adaptation, new translation and innovative stage direction, as will be seen in Brecht's reworking of Gay's play. The threats posed by mass media, already introduced, may be less remediable. In the age of internet streaming and cable television, 'live' performance often means 'live when first recorded'. Satire's capacity to foster a conspiracy against adversaries which actors and spectators share in a theatre space – their unmediated contact, unobstructed by an imaginary fourth wall between them – gives way to studio cameramen and control booth editors deciding what to show viewers. Sound editors decide what is heard on the microphone or bleeped out. Most limiting of all: televised routines often have to stop after a certain amount of time or they will interfere with commercials purchased by program sponsors. Even non-commercial public stations take breaks to thank their sponsors these days.

In deference to their program's commercial interruptions, satiric television sketches on the American program *Saturday Night Live* last about five minutes each. A studio audience of hundreds watches in person, the rest of the audience watches from home in small, separated groups. It could be argued this is the state of popular satire today: watched privately by most spectators, the program comprises short sketches separated by advertisements for expensive cars, drugs and new Hollywood films. Sometimes a celebrity, an American presidential candidate or a famous actor, participates as a guest performer and reads quips from a teleprompter. By contrast, as a way to assess the diminution of satire, consider that Aristophanes in Athens could expect thousands attending the first performance of *The Frogs*, *The Clouds* or *The Knights* to sit outdoors in a large amphitheatre and watch his actors for hours. The performance length allowed for detailed, sustained comic forays with song, dance and repeated mockery of prominent citizens. Audiences did more than applaud. In *The Knights* the chorus leader recalls that the playwright Magnes was 'booed off the stage... because his powers of mockery had deserted him', and the writer Crates had to endure 'violent rebuffs' (Aristophanes 1998: 297–9). Substantial audience size gave spectators the power to disapprove of an author; if he did not lead them to laugh at miscreants, he risked rejection himself. Although devised for one performance only, satire staged in the Theatre of Dionysus could make a lasting impression, given its length, rarity and the many witnesses. In some cases the impression has lasted 2,500 years despite the originally limited run of one day. Writing for a single performance, Aristophanes did not have to worry about his play's topical references going out of date. Satire was here and now, live and in person. Now it is rarely here, at least not in live stage plays.

Satura, Satyr and Satire

Ancient Athenian theatre presented some 'satyr' plays with actors portraying mythical creatures, half-man, half-goat. The only surviving complete Greek satyr text, *The Cyclops* (*c.* 425 BCE) of Euripides, places mythical goat-men on stage to mock the epic heroism of Odysseus as he and the satyrs defy their captor, the Cyclops. The short mythological comedy was devised as an afterpiece to follow a trilogy of tragedies; it should not be confused with the full-length plays of Aristophanes, who placed no satyrs onstage. But the satyrs played a role in the etymology of 'satire', contributing their name to the English word.

Linking modern usage of the word to past practice by satirists, Robert C. Elliott notes that 'our *satire* is derived from Latin *satura* (which had the original sense of *mixture* or *medley*), while our *satirize* and *satirical* come from the Greek word for *satyr*' (1960: 102). Elliott traces the use of satiric invective from early Western poets who preceded Greek theatre to Aristophanic comedy and later satire, where maledictions recited to expel enemies, as well as ancient rituals to invoke fertility, took increasingly comic and theatrical form when characters exchanged insults on stage. Satiric poetry written in Rome by Horace and Juvenal later influenced playwrights too. Early in the seventeenth century, Juvenalian railing could be heard in Ben Jonson's satires *Bartholomew Fair* and *The Alchemist* and John Marston's *The Malcontent*. Shakespeare also knew Juvenal's kind of satire, as he proved by writing scathing curses for Thersites in his Trojan War play, *Troilus and Cressida*. 'I would thou didst itch from head to foot, and I had the scratching of thee; I would make thee the loathsom'st scab in Greece', Thersites informs Ajax, demonstrating the humour and threats of harm contained in satiric invective (1960: 723).

When ancient satirists directed wit and mockery at persons of wealth, power, fame or fashion, their art had the capacity to criticize and shame human subjects through risible depiction. Elliott, in *The Power of Satire*, argues that ridicule constituted an influential form of public disapproval in a 'culture of shame' whose society relied 'on external sanctions to govern behavior', unlike a 'culture of guilt' where 'an individual will obey internalized standards of morality without reference to outside forces' (1960: 67). In our time those 'internalized standards of morality' appear to have been vanquished by self-promoting celebrities, very stable geniuses (as a recent

President said of himself) and their highly paid lawyers who never acknowledge they could be at fault. They have no sense of shame, it seems. Jonathan Swift's admonition that satire is a glass in which the viewer sees everyone but himself needs to be revised; high-placed viewers in contemporary society see only themselves in the glass, and without fault. If the mirror does not flatter, they find another one.

By contrast, when one character in *The Knights* prepares to outwit his rival in debate, he first acknowledges his shortcomings as a shameless speaker. He asks the 'demons of Puffery, Quackery, Foolery, Chicanery, and Debauchery' to give him 'boldness, a ready tongue, and a shameless voice!' so he can defeat his opponent (Aristophanes 1998: 307). This request made by a sausage seller is granted. A surge of arrogance and trickery enables him to defeat a leather merchant named Paphlagon, who in many ways resembles the demagogue Cleon. *The Knights* and a few of Aristophanes's other satires offended Cleon to the extent that the Athenian statesman harassed the playwright and sought his expulsion from the city. He had a sense of shame; but he didn't surrender to it. Like Cleon, some other leaders under attack have acknowledged the efficacy of satire by responding with public objections, prosecution of the artists and government censorship. Keeping Aristophanes company in this history of stage satire's repression are Molière, John Gay, Henry Fielding, Bertolt Brecht, Nicolai Erdman, Mikhail Bulgakov, Joan Littlewood and Dario Fo; all found themselves legally challenged, censored or had their productions closed in unsought, backhanded tributes to the power of their satiric and provocative theatre. If their art was harmless, they might have been left alone; but the history of satire would be poorer, deprived of testimony to the effective ridicule in their plays.

Quite often the same authorities who repressed satire first inspired it. Juvenal, in the first century CE, confessed that actual events, disquieting behaviour by contemporaries, compelled him to write. How could he not write satire, asked the Roman poet, given all the ridiculous and upsetting events he witnessed in the imperial capital. 'Satire? What else... How can you help but fill whole notebooks?' he wondered (in Rolf Humphries's translation), as he cited egregious, satire-susceptible actions: 'Vice is at its peak. Set sail, O writer of Satire.' Juvenal questioned whether he must 'always be listening [to others at fault] and not pay them back?' and decided to repay offenders through satiric verse. He wrote no plays, perhaps because he agreed with one character in his poetry who complains that in 'Greekized Rome', 'Greece is a stage and every Greek an actor' (Juvenal 1958: 17–22, 35, 37). His view that corruption, greed and lies lend themselves to satire, almost compose stage satire themselves, and actual events serve as a primary source for his complaints, elucidates practices found in playwriting from Aristophanes in ancient Athens to Dario Fo in modern-day Milan. These satirists place on stage characters who have living counterparts. The writers quote, paraphrase and recontextualize the language of their subjects to comic effect. Names and specific offenses may be altered in their plays; but at the time of performance, audiences know who and what are targeted. In *The Plot of Satire,* Alvin Kernan describes the trajectory of this creative process: 'scenes of idiocy and greed which [satirists] construct are not... the products of misanthropy, but the work of serious artists trying to catch the grotesque shapes toward which human form and the world are being forced under the weight of stupidity' (1965: 5).

These 'grotesque' shapes take particular human forms in theatre, as they must when embodied by actors. Not every character in the plays is based on a well-known person. Sometimes a preposterous figure represents a composite. He or she is an allegorical figure or archetype given specific traits; but veiled and allegorical satire has proven as controversial as direct assault. When Molière portrayed an imposter as a religious minister in *Tartuffe* (1664, revised 1667), the Archbishop of Paris called for a ban on the play. Father Roulle of St. Barthelemy Church said the play and its author should be burnt. Molière named no particular, living clergyman; but churchmen accused the playwright himself of impiety, and saw the play as a broadside against their religion rather than a portrait of one character's religious hypocrisy. Larry Norman suggests that Molière's 'shrewd manipulation of the audience's sense of self-recognition' allowed him to 'develop satire that deftly mixed the particular with the general, the individual and the universal' (2006: 60) (Figure 1). Rewritten after the initial objections, *Tartuffe* was approved by France's reigning monarch, if not its churchmen. The play includes an homage to the king whose representative rescues Tartuffe's victims. (Molière was one of those victims, in a sense, as his career was endangered by adversaries.) His Highness King Louis XIV does not appear in the play; but the text makes him omniscient or at least well-informed. Aware of the title character's crimes, the monarch's agent arrests the villain and informs those rescued: 'With one keen glance, the King perceived the whole/Perverseness and corruption of [Tartuffe's] soul' (1982: 324). Leading cardinals and other high church officials are not seen or heard in this

MOLIERE LISANT SON TARTUFFE CHEZ NINON DE L'ENCLOS

Figure 1 *Molière reads* Tartuffe *free of censors in a Parisian salon.*

resolution. Molière silences them, keeps them off his stage, as it were, after their earlier attacks forced him to change the script.

In *Tartuffe* most of the title character's hypocrisy, blackmail and sexual overtures can be understood by a modern audience without knowing details about the church in Molière's day. In the satirist's own time, such details seem to have been read between the lines by his contemporaries. Molière himself said that *Tartuffe* was 'a play that has created quite a stir and that has been persecuted for some time; the people it portrays have shown themselves to be more powerful in France than all those I have portrayed hitherto' (Norman 2006: 59). The affront posed by his satire in 1664 is far less likely to be experienced now if staged without changes in its text. Like satires by Aristophanes and Jonson, *Tartuffe* now could be regarded as a museum piece, a classic that refers to a world far removed from that of a modern audience. The Russian satirist Mikhail Bulgakov found a way to make this material more provocative and timely when he wrote a new play about Molière and *Tartuffe. Molière: A Cabal of Hypocrites* was banned by Soviet authorities in 1930, then allowed to open in 1936, then withdrawn from the Moscow Art Theatre after seven performances. Stalin's ever-watchful advisors seem to have read references to the Soviet Union into lines such as Molière's warning to his beloved Armande: 'I'm surrounded by enemies', although in context the line refers to an artist's fear of betrayal in love, not fear of political arrest (1991: 239). Classical satire lived anew for seven performances, but only seven performances, after Bulgakov inventively reutilized an old plot, its characters and theatre history. Stalin secretly endorsed the decision to close Bulgakov's play in 1936, according to Anatoly Smeliansky; one of the dictator's censors said the play invited 'the theatregoer to see an analogy between the situation of a writer under the dictatorship of the proletariat and the "tyranny without redress" under Louis XIV'. Evidently no one at the Moscow Art Theatre noticed this alleged subversion during the play's four years of intermittent rehearsal; but Stalin detected the threat without attending a performance

– he merely read and approved a recommendation from the Chairman of the Committee for the Arts to ban a play that had 'stray[ed] from the line of socialist realism' (Smeliansky 1993: 260).

Molière's *Tartuffe*, Bulgakov's *Molière* and other plays attest that stage satire can upset civic, religious, military and cultural leaders without mentioning their names. Conventions of allegory and historical drama allow for lively inference of contemporary misconduct. Given sufficient clues, audiences will guess or try to recognize those accused of malfeasance. Aristophanes provided such clues. The living tyrant Cleon is named only once, incidentally, in *The Knights*; but his stand-in known as Paphlagon throughout the play was a character whose off-stage counterpart Athenian audiences had no difficulty recognizing.

The Art of Satiric Impersonation

A well-known public leader like Cleon supplied Aristophanes not only with speeches to adapt and distort through parody, but also a physical appearance to mimic. Actor impersonation is a kind of quotation. Brecht would later call for his actors to create 'quotable gestures' (1957: 138). In a satiric scene, Brecht wrote in *The Resistible Rise of Arturo Ui*, discussed later, the gangster Ui asks an actor to teach him gestures that will improve his public speaking. Hitler himself is said to have done this, but less humorously. In *Arturo Ui* and other satires, by assuming the body type, voice or face (thanks to mask and prosthetics) of a well-known person, an actor physically links life outside the theatre to that on stage. A satiric impersonator more or less captures his 'enemy', steps into an opponent's body and holds it hostage.

The hostage-taking became literal in one of Italian satirist Dario Fo's plays, where he imagined the kidnapping of a prominent Italian, Fiat automobile magnate Gianni Agnelli.

After the character's face changed due to an accident that required plastic surgery, the audience was free to see the man with Fo's face as that of wealthy playboy and industrialist Agnelli, whatever he looked like. The fact that author Fo himself portrayed the Fiat magnate onstage made the impersonation doubly ironic, as the satirist became the man he wanted to ridicule. Fo pretended to suffer the indignities he imposed on his antagonist in *Trumpets and Raspberries*. Based in part on the 1978 kidnapping of Italian Prime Minister Aldo Moro, Fo's satire did not end with the hostage executed, as the Red Brigades executed Moro. Instead he let a famous industrialist celebrate his survival and proclaim (through Fo's voice) himself more powerful than a Prime Minister. Having fully recovered from amnesia and surgery, and revelling in his identity, Fo's Agnelli announced: 'Moro was sacrificed in order to save the respectability of the aforementioned financial state... How could they think of sacrificing me, in order to save the state. I am the state!' (1984: 68). Praising himself with comic excess, Fo's Agnelli echoed the boast of another wealthy industrialist, Undershaft in Shaw's *Major Barbara*, who claimed the government followed his orders and went to war for his profit. For most of Fo's satire, however, the author, and not Agnelli, ruled; the captured financier had to do whatever his impersonator and satirist demanded. Cleon in Athens may well have had a comparable experience, and it is said that Aristophanes himself played the tyrant's role onstage.

If audiences today do not know much about Cleon's demagoguery in Athens or the false accusations of terrorism made against activists in Agnelli's Italy, they are going to be lost sometime during performances of *The Knights* and *Trumpets and Raspberries*. Actors rehearsing these plays learn (if they don't already know) about the individuals they portray – their voices, bodies, biographies – to prepare for their roles. Ideally audiences, too, are prepared for the satire, having lived in the same world and heard complaints, praise and gossip about Cleon, Agnelli or other prominent citizens subjected to ridicule. *An Actor Prepares*, the book of instruction Stanislavsky wrote for actors, might deserve a sequel, *An Audience Prepares*, that would offer the public advice on stage satires they are about to see.

Impersonation of a national leader is not the only way to create satire on stage; nor is it always an effective method. The 1937 American musical *I'd Rather Be Right*, by Kaufman and Hart, featured an actor impersonating President Franklin D. Roosevelt, then serving his second term in office; but the musical's plot, in which FDR tries to balance his government's budget and improve the economy so a young couple can afford to marry, hardly looks at the President's own programs. Facilitating a wedding becomes his highest priority. The love story diverts attention from the world off-stage and its leaders, rather than allowing the play to confront the economic and social crises faced during the Great Depression; the result is an innocuous romantic comedy with famous name characters.

The moment an actor or spectator makes a connection between life on stage and an off-stage counterpart is central to the experience satiric theatre offers its audience. Alvin Kernan discounts the importance of specific and topical references when he writes:

> However various the accents spoken by the men and women who inhabit satire, however different the clothing they wear, the streets they walk, and the cities they dirty, they exert the same kind of pressure on society and nature, and create the same kind of world (1965: 22).

If this were the case, detailed references in plays by Aristophanes, Jonson, Fo and others would not become arcane and need footnotes or new translations. More important, without such detail satirists could not give the persons they ridicule thorough exposure as miscreants and fools. To take on the abusive power of a leader, the playwright offers a copy of it. Scrupulous attention to the life of an unscrupulous tyrant enabled Aristophanes to ridicule Cleon in *The Knights*, considered in the next chapter.

2

Aristophanes and After: Origins and Legacy of Ancient Athenian Satire

Modern scholars describe Aristophanes as the author of 'Old Comedy' or 'Attic Comedy', which immediately makes his plays sound timeworn, if not ancient, when in fact they were new and innovative when staged in the fifth century BCE. Closer to his own age, when his writing was less than a century old, Aristophanes (*c.* 450 BCE–388 BCE) received brief mention in the lectures of Aristotle. In *The Poetics* (*c.* 335 BCE), the Greek philosopher refers to 'Comedy' and 'Tragedy' as the two major forms of dramatic poetry, and notes that Aristophanes imitates 'persons acting and doing', meaning he writes plays (1961: 52–3). *The Poetics* looks far more closely at the structure of tragedy than comedy, and never discusses satire as a separate form of theatre. This could explain why other later analysts deferential to Aristotle see Old Comedy where they could see satire.

If critical authority is needed to support use of the term 'satire' in a discussion of Aristophanes, we might turn to Jonathan Swift, who knew the classics and the art of satire well. Although he does not mention Aristophanes in his *Account of a Battel between the Antient and Modern Books* or a later discussion of *The Beggar's Opera*, he helpfully refers to satire in theatre a number of times. First he calls John Gay's play a 'comedy or farce (or whatever name the critics will allow it)'. Then Swift praises 'humour' as the 'best ingredient toward the kind of satire which is most useful' as it 'laughs Men out of their Follies and Vices', phrases suggesting the art is purgative or corrective. Swift also argues that 'corruption in religion, politics, and law may be proper topics for this kind of satire' (1730: 21–2, 28). Humorous exposure of corruption, vice and folly like that Swift noted in *The Beggar's Opera* also occurs in the plays of Jonson, Molière, Gogol, Brecht, Behan and Fo, which doesn't make them all equal or the same; but all of these playwrights deserve to be recognized, along with Aristophanes, as authors of 'satire which is most useful'.

If Aristophanes's plays often have been called comedies rather than satires, it could be due to their historical antecedent in the *Komos*, a Greek word for processional revelry that preceded play competitions. *Komos* has been defined by Alexis Solomos as an 'antique carnival' in which worshippers of the god Dionysus 'dressed up in every imaginable kind of droll or weird disguise' (1974: 34). The comic role-playing in these ancient processions may have inspired Aristophanes and the later description of his plays as comedies. M. S. Silk, in *Aristophanes and the Definition of Comedy*, prefers to see comedy rather than satire at the centre of most of the plays. He concedes that one of the author's texts, *The Clouds*, is a work 'of which we can truly say that satire is at its heart'. But Silk declines to see this form as the core of other plays by Aristophanes because 'satire is essentially moral – and negative... deficiencies... are held up to ridicule. Satire invites, and perhaps promotes, dissatisfaction. In this sense, all Aristophanes' plays include some satire, but only in *Clouds* is satire dominant.' The other plays by Aristophanes are not negative enough to qualify as complete satires in Silk's view. In *The Knights*, the demagogue Cleon's 'perverse genius is celebrated, as much as satirized', according to Silk (2000: 368). That might be disputed. If affirmations surface once in a while in the play, that is only to be expected; an art that is going to tear down or demean men in high places first has to consider the heights and their occupants. As the chorus leader says in *The Knights*: 'There's nothing invidious about calling bad people names; it's a way to honor good people, if you stop to think about it' (1998: 389). Cleon is called a lot of names, rarely his own, as will be seen.

Even if Aristophanes was not called a satirist by Aristotle or some modern scholars, his plays provide examples of popular and socially ameliorative stage performance achieved through satire. City-state festivals sponsored by the government and wealthy patrons granted authors licence to write irreverently about contemporary leaders, crises and fashions. Playwrights competed for prizes at the Lenaea (winter festival first held 440 BCE) and at the City or Great Dionysia (spring festival that first staged tragedies in 534 BCE, added comedies in 486 BCE). Ostensibly dedicated to Dionysus, a god of wine, fertility and theatre, the festivals offered war-weary citizens a holiday with song, dance, jokes and – in *The Knights* and other plays – peace treaties. The City Dionysia presented three comic plays on the same day, and three days of tragic trilogies. Tragedians looked at mythological and Homeric figures, and not the war actually going on from 431 to 404 BCE, while satirists like Aristophanes referred to the Peloponnesian war and lives of persons present and known in Athens, as well as invented characters. Only eleven plays by Aristophanes survive; although hundreds of scripts were written by him and his competitors, no more than fragments of the others have been preserved. At the start of this survey it was noted satire is an endangered species; it was endangered early, nearly lost, thousands of years ago, but some of the Greek plays were preserved.

Ordering Disorder

In the Athenian satires that survive, as well as later satiric plays, oppositional references to men in power, samples of egregious behaviour and plans for peace are shaped into scenes of farcical, grotesque and absurd action. Colourful language delivered in song and spoken dialogue goes beyond the reality that inspired it. That reality may be comic and unruly to begin with, from the satirist's perspective; but without artful construction, these plays would not have the focus, extended comedy and cumulative impact that made them popular. The comic anarchy they let loose breaks through a particular, orderly structure.

Aristophanes centres each of his satires around an *agon*, Greek for debate or conflict, one of several structural components that allows those satirized to be verbally and physically attacked. First the play opens with a prologue (*proagon*) that introduces the circumstances in need of change, and the men or women who want to change it. *The Knights* begins with two discontent slaves complaining of oppression caused by a third slave, Paphlagon, who manipulates their master, Demos. The *proagon* here, as in other Aristophanic satires, has characters initiate a scheme to improve their lives. After some false starts, the oppressed slaves read an oracle and decide it means Paphlagon will be overtaken by a newcomer. The predicted successor, a sausage seller, arrives and the two discontent slaves encourage him to debate their nemesis.

Ancient Greek satire as well as tragedy usually had no more than three actors on stage at once – not counting members of the chorus. The actors wore masks and by changing them could play a large number of roles during the performance. In *The Knights*, two characters (Paphlagon and the sausage seller) hold the stage for many scenes – termed *episodes* in Greek – separated by *stasima* or choral songs.

The conversation between a pair of slaves in the first scene, followed by debate between two characters (sausage seller and Paphlagon), exemplifies a pattern of comic dialogue found in other plays by Aristophanes. Two Athenian exiles plan for a new life away from taxes and war in *The Birds*. Dionysus with his servant Xanthias reveals early in *The Frogs* his plan to travel to Hades in search of a deceased playwright. The comic patter between two men in these scenes anticipates the routines of modern vaudeville teams, the filmed comedy of Laurel and Hardy, as well as Estragon and Vladimir entertaining one another in *Waiting for Godot*.

Following the *proagon* and introduction of lead characters, the chorus's entrance (*parados*) brings on stage the title characters of *The Knights*, twenty-four men who dance and comment on the action through their songs and occasional speech. Jeffrey Henderson compares their choral verse to the rhymed songs devised by Gilbert and Sullivan (Aristophanes 1998: 24). They danced their formations in the *orchestra*, a performance space that lead character actors shared at times.

Towards the middle of the play, Aristophanes introduces a direct address to the audience (*parabasis*) delivered by the chorus leader. The *parabasis* praises the play and its creators, and offers commentary on political and social situations. While other satires by Aristophanes had one *parabasis*, *The Knights* has two. Characters also turn to spectators and briefly address them elsewhere in the play.

During the *parabasis* only the chorus leader spoke, pleading for a festival prize and other concessions, criticizing selected citizens, appraising Athenian government policy. In some of Aristophanes's satires, a *parabasis* delivered with humour but not entirely in jest called for action outside the theatre. Citing his duty to determine the best course for the city, the chorus leader in *The Frogs* (405 BCE) proposed political amnesty for Alcibiades and other men who could help Athens at a time when it was faring badly in the Peloponnesian war. The proposal in that *parabasis* proved so popular that *The Frogs* was given a second performance, a rare occurrence.

In *The Knights* the first of two *parabases* begins with praise of the playwright. The chorus leader explains that Aristophanes gave his own name, risking the loss of reputation that may follow, when he sought a chorus for this production. (Someone else hired his choruses for earlier plays.) The address also praises horsemen and their selfless valour in war, hinting other warriors are not as commendable. A second *parabasis* concerns ships under the command of Hyperbolus and declares him unfit to lead. Leadership of Athens is questioned elsewhere in the play too, of course.

Winning by a Hare

Throughout this satire, Aristophanes looks critically at a city-state troubled by war and threats to its democratic rule. Some troubles are resolved in the closing scenes. Each of his plays concludes with a wedding, feast, peace treaty or other cause for celebration that precedes the exit (*exodus*) of the chorus and others from the performance space. In *The Knights* a feast follows Demos's offer of victory to the contestant who delivers the best meal. The sausage seller steals a jugged hare from his rival and sees his act as a fitting sequel to Paphlagon's theft of credit for a military victory in Pylos.

Paphlagon: Damn it all, you pinched my hare! That's unfair.

Sausage Seller: By Poseidon, it isn't. I'm just imitating you with the men from Pylos.

(1998: 379)

Their fight over food is more humorous and less harmful than wartime manoeuvres abroad. In some ancient rituals offerings were burnt in honour of the gods. Here Demos ('the people'), putative master of the rival slaves, is the beneficiary of the offerings: 'putative' master because the slaves rule their master and take charge of events for most of the play.

There is no wedding at the end of *The Knights*, but a prize of two women goes to Demos. The two 'beautiful girls' are said to be thirty-year peace treaties previously hidden by Paphlagon. After the sausage seller gives the newly found 'treaties' to Demos, the master asks if he can 'lay them down and ratify them' (1998: 403). Treatment of the women as sex objects, not so funny from a modern perspective, could have amused patriarchal Athenians, whose culture has been called phallocentric. Like the state, theatrical satire was male-dominated (Figure 2). Patriarchs received some resistance in Aristophanic satires such as *Lysistrata, Women at the Thesmophoria* and *The Assembly of Women*, where female characters objected to men's warfare, discriminatory treatment and the unflattering depiction of women on stage. Since the Greek women on stage were portrayed by male actors in roles scripted by men, the scenes of protest may have mocked the protesters along with male chauvinism. In modern productions of Aristophanes, if women are cast and perform with their own faces instead of masks, their speeches in *Lysistrata* could take on a new tenor more critical of men. But the women in *The Knights* do not speak at all.

The 'peace treaties' brought on stage in 424 BCE probably would have been men wearing pale, women's face masks. The

Figure 2 *A dance from Aristophanes's* Peace *staged by Benno Besson in Berlin, 1962.*

kind of risqué humour their entrance elicits was later lightly disparaged by Jonathan Swift in a poem he sent his friend Thomas Sheridan: 'But as to comic Aristophanes, / The rogue's too bawdy and too prophane is' (Swift 1801: unpaged). Jokes about women's sexual activity and private parts arise far more in other satires than in *The Knights*; but that did not prevent Hellenist Max Pohlenz from seeing the reference to a thirty-year peace treaty as a call to fill the stage with thirty nude dancing girls. Rather than Pohlenz's female chorus line, only 'one maiden alone, beautiful maybe, but not nude' was required for the scene, so that Demos 'gets one girl and no more' in Fernando Russo's reading (1994: 84). In any case, no consummation is enacted, and peace, whatever its quantity and gender, does not stay long. The play ends with the cheerful departure of Demos, his treaties and slaves, followed by a choral *exodus*. Paphlagon, having fainted on stage, is revived and led off separately, visibly no longer a leader.

Aristophanic satires follow a set structure; but compared to Roman comedy their sequence of scenes is less linear, more open-ended, as intruders enter and digressions occur. In *The Knights* the *parabases* and episodes separated by choral song allow for special pleadings and changes of tack. At one point Demos asks Paphlagon to return his ring and end service as his steward. The contest would seem to be over with the sausage seller victorious. But it continues after Paphlagon begs for another chance.

One common link between Greek and Roman comedy is their propensity to allow slaves and women freedoms that subvert hierarchical order. Slavery and the subservience of women to men in ancient times were not inherently comic topics; but a departure from normalcy in these plays allows the oppressed to take exceptional actions. The slaves who serve their masters often do so through devious and illicit manoeuvres. In *The Knights* as two discontent slaves take the initiative, find and encourage a successor (the sausage seller) to Paphlagon, their agency lets spectators see Athens from the perspective of disempowered men seeking change. Henderson argues that Aristophanes criticized the status quo by viewing it 'through the eyes of ordinary people or people ordinarily excluded from public power, like women' (Aristophanes 1996: 12). This is not to say that Aristophanes wanted to give women or slaves greater freedom and power outside the theatre; but in the service of satire he allowed them liberties. They transgressed, temporarily took charge, became advocates for a different society through their abnormal and comic action. In *The Knights*, the scheme initiated by two slaves ends with the third slave, the bully Paphlagon, sent 'where all his friends / All his victims, can go and laugh at him' (1993: 126). This is a goal of satire: to turn a tyrant into a laughing stock. Paphlagon is sentenced to sell food at the city gates. A pun suggests he 'made a hash' of his reign, and he is going to make another kind of hash by working as a sausage seller at the edge of the city, where foreigners can see the humiliated man at they could not at the Lenaea.

Allegory, History, Prophecy

To advance his comic vision, Aristophanes employs allegory, history and prophecy, all of which make *The Knights* more than topical satire. Through allegory *The Knights* distances the action from realistic representation of Athenian leadership in 424 BCE, and places characters in a fictitious situation that at times parallels off-stage life, but is not the same as it. Questions about democratic rule and resistance to threats posed by Cleon come through exaggerated portraits of the allegorical characters. Demos represents 'the people' – Athenian citizenry and its aggregate, those who participate in the Assembly. Paphlagon represents Cleon, and initially Demos favours him, unaware of his slave's abusive behaviour. The other two slaves who serve Demos and want to see Paphlagon defeated are given the names of two Athenian generals: Demosthenes and Nicias. Russo argues that these two servants 'procrastinate selfishly and abdicate [taking action] precisely because they are caricatures of Demosthenes and Nikias', who hesitated to take military action in Pylos (1994: 80). Solomos speculates the two generals themselves sat in the audience, enjoying 'the anti-Cleonic gags more than anybody else' (1974: 92).

The allegory concludes after the sausage-seller proves to be coarser and more removed from civility than his opponent, in an Athens not unlike Washington, DC in recent years, or any other place where rule of law gives way to crude and misleading political manoeuvres. After the sausage vendor's victory in the contest with Paphlagon, however, he becomes a model citizen; virtue triumphs, although it arrives without spectators seeing how or why the victor is transformed. He also claims to have transformed Demos. A less allegorical structure might require another scene towards the end, to show the education of the contest winner – his progression from lying and theft to civic responsibility. But this is not a realistic or naturalistic play. There was ample basis in Athenian life for the fantasy. The girls who represent the thirty-year peace treaties hidden by Paphlagon, for example, had a living counterpart in Sparta's interest in a peace treaty dismissed by Cleon.

Contrary to the play's optimistic ending, Aristophanes's own view of peace prospects may have been more fully expressed in the first *parabasis,* where the chorus leader says that the knights want to fight for the city and its gods, and if peace ever comes, they ask only for permission to wear their hair long and bathe in luxury. Peace's arrival is not predicted at that point, and few benefits from it are asked.

The allegory omits Cleon's name (with one minor exception around line 975); but a one-to-one correspondence between him and Paphlagon is implied throughout. This allows the play to offer historically based comic criticism of an Athenian demagogue. While the first audience could catch references to Cleon and other Greeks without mention of their names, those allusions might not be followed by a modern audience unless it reads notes. When the sausage seller says that Paphlagon 'has reaped what another man sowed, and now wants to sell off the ears of corn' MacDowell notes 'that is obviously an allegorical reference to Kleon's getting credit for the success at Pylos after Demosthenes had done most of the work, and it implies that he [Kleon] hopes to get money for releasing the Spartan prisoners' (1995: 99). It may not be obvious to a modern audience.

Although *The Knights* is not a history play, some dialogue anticipates chapters recorded later (*c.* 404 BCE) in Thucydides's history of the Peloponnesian war. Cleon was the subject of laughter there too. Before the tyrant chose his military partner, writes Thucydides, Cleon 'claimed that within twenty days he would either bring the Spartans [on the island of Pylos] back to Athens or would kill them on the spot. This irresponsible claim caused a certain amount of laughter' (1972: 283). Similar irresponsible boasting can be heard in *The Knights*, and the audience's recognition of its resemblance to Cleon's pre-invasion boasting could have prompted a certain amount of laughter again. Paphlagon anticipates comparison between himself and Cleon as he announces: 'I'd like to know who in the world you compare me with! Me. I'll polish off a plateful of hot tuna right now, wash it down with a pitcher of neat wine, and then screw the generals at Pylos!' (1998: 275). Whether he means to screw enemy generals or his own out of victory, his comic vows draw on Cleon's promise to win in Pylos. The feast Paphlagon consumes here before victory might be seen as premature acceptance of the special meals to which triumphant Athenian generals were entitled, along with a reward of front-row seating in the theatre.

Cleon's rejection of a peace offer also receives recognition – without an allegorical name given to him – in Thucydides's historical account: 'The man who, more than the others, encouraged them in this attitude [of withholding agreement in a peace treaty] was Cleon' (1972: 277). When Cleon returned to Athens with 292 Spartan hostages after victory in Pylos, he refused to negotiate a peace treaty with the enemy, to the dismay of Aristophanes. Thirty-one years of peace and a thirty-year treaty of peace preceded the beginning of the

Peloponnesian war in 431 BCE. The ending of *The Knights*, with delivery of two thirty-year peace treaties, keeps the play in the realm of allegory, but recalls the prior, greatly missed history of peace.

Thucydides also casts doubt on Cleon's achievement of victory at Pylos. The *History of the Peloponnesian War* reports 'the original plan made by Demosthenes for the landing' at Pylos was put into operation when Cleon arrived, but Cleon chose to have Demosthenes 'as his colleague, because he heard that he was already planning to make a landing on the island' (1972: 283). Without calling Cleon a thief, Thucydides gives General Demosthenes some credit for the victory. Aristophanes gives Demosthenes more credit, and Cleon less for stealing victory from his colleague.

The Athenian tyrant has not always been a laughingstock. A 1987 article by Ian Worthington defends the general and claims his rejection of Spartan peace proposals was warranted. Aristophanes in *The Knights* barely mentions Cleon's aversion to a peace treaty, Worthington contends, because the satirist knew the agreement would not bring lasting peace (1987: 56–7). Contrary to Worthington, the playwright is not so restrained in his language (with talk about butt-kicking and paper-ripping) when he has the sausage seller accuse Paphlagon of placing self-interest above his country's, and preferring bribes to peace proposals.

> **Sausage Seller:** … when Archeptolemus brought a peace proposal you tore it in pieces, and the embassies that offered a treaty, you kicked their butts and drove them from the city …. [and figured out] how you can steal and take bribes from the allied cities.
>
> (1998: 327–8)

Before the play named after them opened, the knights had accused Cleon of taking bribes from allies (Solomos 1974: 91). The playwright did not have to invent this charge for his allegory.

Ancient Athenian history also can be glimpsed in the play's depiction of tradesmen as leaders. It was 'historical fact', Victor Ehrenberg observes, that by the time of *The Knights* 'leading politicians [such as Cleon] belonged to the middle-class of business men. They gradually displaced the aristocratic leaders, the men "from the great houses"' (1962: 210). The knights in the play want to trade one coarse speaker with merchant-class background for another, but Aristophanes himself regrets the loss of past leadership that was more aristocratic. The ascent of middle-class businessmen in the play reflects changes in society; but the playwright's misgivings about the change can be seen too, particularly when Demos undergoes a transformation and turns Periclean late in the play.

The possibility of worsening government leadership is reversed in the closing scene as the chorus declares that Demos, freed from Paphlagon, now lives in an Athens returned to its old greatness. The satirist restores some of the old order, at least a sign of it. Demos re-enters rejuvenated and dressed in clothing associated with the earlier age of Periclean rule. 'He lives in the violet-crowned Athens of old.' He is 'wearing a golden cricket' and looks 'resplendent in his old time costume', we are told, as if it is not enough to let the audience see the change; they have to hear about it too (Aristophanes 1998: 395–7). Perhaps spectators in the back rows would not have seen the gold brooch's detail from their distance. MacDowell argues that the 'cicada brooch' was fashionable 'in the days of the Persian Wars', and it appears as a sign of the author's 'nostalgia for the good old days' (1995: 104–5). Wars were fought under Pericles, too; but none as devastating and lengthy as the Peloponnesian war still going on when *The Knights* opened. Douglas Parker clarifies the contrast between old and new leaders when he notes that while Aristophanes as 'a conservative' 'distinguishes clearly between Perikles and his corrupt successors, he nonetheless hold Perikles responsible for creating the political system in which men like Kleon could thrive' (in Aristophanes 1969: 110). Aristophanes's invocation of the old aristocratic order suggests why Dario Fo described the Greek satirist as a 'reactionary not bereft of talent' (1987: 184).

Fo may be right; but at the same time satire in *The Knights*
favours democracy (limited though it may have been) in the
character of Demos. The playwright's preference for an older
order led him to ridicule the demagogue of the new one.

Besides appraising Athenian history, *The Knights* introduces
prophecy. In the play's first *parabasis*, a speech argues that the
author 'dares to say what's right and nobly strides forth against
the typhoon and the whirlwind' (1998: 295). The speech
makes a case for the satirist as a prophet who articulates what
others refuse to see or are unable to say in public. Cleon's
ascendency is the whirlwind, and *The Knights* says so in its
own way. Within the play oracles are read aloud. Some are
mocked, some fulfilled; but all of them require characters to
look towards the future and call for change, oracular vision of
a comic variety.

After one of Demos's slaves reads an oracle about sellers of
tripe and sausage, the insurgent vendor asks how it applies to
him, and an Aesopian answer follows. Animal imagery describes
Paphlagon as a 'rawhide eagle' who 'snatches and takes' with
'crooked hands' and will be overpowered by a newcomer
(1998: 257). This prediction previews the remainder of the
plot; by setting up later scenes this way, the author ensures
his characters' fates will end as ordained. He also offers very
funny praise of the future victor when the First Slave informs
the sausage seller: 'You've got everything a demagogue needs:
repulsive voice, low birth, marketplace morals – you've got all
the ingredients for a political career' (1998: 259). Under the
auspices of prophecy, this speech ridicules the tyrant sitting in
the front row of the amphitheatre. Translator Henderson adds
a stage direction that has the bearer of the oracle pointing to
Cleon when he speaks of an eagle, in case the object of the
reference or the audience doesn't know who is the snatcher
(1988: 257). The scene is allegory and direct reference at the
same time.

The three perspectives of allegory, history and prophecy
fuse in *The Knights*, as the allegory about restoration of
democracy includes satire of Cleon's past activity and follows

the prophesized path of a change in leadership. Attribution of Cleon's behaviour to a character named Paphlagon gives the playwright licence to confound reality with caricature at the same time he draws on recent history in references to the Peloponnesian war and Athenian government.

Calling in the Cavalry

Another component of the play drawn from Athenian life is the group featured in the play's title. The chorus of knights enters in response to a slave's call for cavalry aid. A mêlée ensues with denunciations and the beating up of Paphlagon. The bully responds with threats and entreaties, and his oratory appears to stem the physical assault. For the rest of the play, the main combatants are the tyrant Paphlagon and the sausage seller. Choral odes and commentary by the knights criticize Paphlagon and praise his opponent. 'How well and adroitly you've mounted your verbal attack!' the chorus leader says of the sausage seller, inadvertently praising the playwright too (1998: 289). Denunciation of the demagogue by the knights in the play, supported by complaints from the sausage seller and the oppressed slaves, makes Cleon's stand-in a minority of one on stage. Off-stage Cleon previously had accused actual knights of refusing to fight in war after they accused him of bribery (Solomos 1974: 91–2). For that reason, actual knights seated in the audience in 424 BCE probably cheered for the sausage vendor and their representatives in the chorus.

While Aristophanes sometimes criticized wealthy men in his satires, he praised them on this occasion. Knights who lived in Athens were rich enough to enter the army with their own horses. MacDowell contends that it would be more appropriate to translate their title and the play's title as 'horsemen' rather than 'knights' (1995: 80); but in either case, the play pays tribute to them. Both the horses and their riders receive favourable recognition in the play's first *parabasis,* where Aristophanes anticipates Swift's attribution of intelligence and language to steeds (called Houyhnhnms by Gulliver). The chorus leader claims that aboard a ship, cavalry horses rowed with oars just like humans and chanted too. These singing horses might have been heard during performance of *The Knights*, if some of the chorus members portrayed them with other men – the knights – mounted on their backs. One preserved Greek vase identified as a depiction of a chorus of knights depicts men wearing masks, helmets and padded uniforms as they sit mounted on other men. This could be how the knights looked on stage (Ehrenberg 1962: Plate 11.b). The sat-upon men wear horse-tails and horse-heads. A musician plays a wind instrument while the human horses with riders dance. The vase painting like the play is far from realistic in its representation. Without referring to this vase, theatre historian Russo suggests that the chorus of twenty-four men in *The Knights* entered 'one as horse, the other as rider… hence, twelve "horses wearing equine masks and tails"… and twelve young-looking, long-haired horsemen' (1994: 88). Other plays by Aristophanes featured choruses of actors representing birds, wasps and frogs; this one could have offered the spectacle of horses engaged in song and dance along with their riders.

Actors Take Over the Government

The knights and Cleon were not the only ones who saw themselves represented on stage in this production. The audience in 424 BCE would have included a large number of other prominent and politically engaged Athenian citizens. Since the play was performed at the Lenaea, a January festival, foreigners were absent, kept away by the difficulties of winter travel. A small number of slaves and women could have been present, and the play has characters representing both of these populations. A majority of the viewers were male citizens, and a sizable number of the men attending *The Knights* were probably members of the Council and Assembly. 'The audience was the Athenian people, the same people who formed the assembly,' writes Victor Ehrenberg of Aristophanic spectators, without noting the full implications of his assertion (1962: 27). The Theatre of Dionysus seated 15,000 to 17,000 people out of a total city-state population of 250,000 (Figure 3). We don't know what percentage of Athens's legislative bodies watched *The Knights*, but there was room for all of the Assembly's 6,000 participants, along with the Council's 500 members (fifty from each of ten tribes), as well as a thousand knights. (The Council has also been called the Senate.) No attendance list survives, and the calculation is speculative. But as leading citizens and men of public affairs, Athenian legislators and knights would have found it hard to resist attending this satiric play. Even if they didn't know in advance that the author would attack Cleon, the Lenaea was a major annual event. What public official wouldn't want to see if he or one of his colleagues

Figure 3 *Ruins of the Theatre of Dionysus, Athens, photographed in 1937. This is not how it looked in 424 BCE.*

was ridiculed? Without question all the Assembly and Council members and knights knew who Cleon was.

Whether or not the entire Assembly watched the play, its body is called into session in *The Knights* around line 744. 'I suggest that you hold an Assembly right away', Paphlagon advises his master so that Demos can determine which slave is most devoted to him (1998: 319). In one sense, Demos *is* the Assembly; he represents the people of Athens. If actual Assembly members were sitting in the audience, their presence too would have been acknowledged in this scene. Henderson in his translation of the scene inserts a stage direction indicating performers should move to the orchestra to 'be in attendance on the Pynx', the site for Assembly sessions (1998: 321). The change relocates actors who begin performance of *The Knights* standing in front of the scene house (*skene*) representing the house of Demos. The debaters move closer to the audience and to Cleon seated in the front row. As the two rivals face Demos, who sits on a rock in the orchestra, they also address the larger audience that fills the amphitheatre behind him; far more than 6,000 Assembly members could be brought into their 'legislative' session, encouraged to applaud and take sides. The chorus of knights continues to cheer the sausage seller on, and later claims it helped him win the contest; but in his effort to impress Demos, the victor also faces an audience of legislators.

He reports an off-stage meeting with legislators earlier in *The Knights*. During the *parabasis*, the sausage vendor has time to exit and he returns to report his victorious manipulation of Council members. If many of the Council's 500 members were in the audience, they would have heard the food vendor boast about his meeting. After cornering the market in coriander and leeks for seasoning sprats, he offered delighted city councillors his tasty bribes. The sausage seller's manoeuvre gave him the whole Council at a small cost, and intentionally distracted councillors from Sparta's offer of a peace treaty. Athens previously may have spurned Spartan peace offers at Cleon's urging; but here the chance to reject peace went to his stand-in's rival. The sausage seller out-Cleons Cleon. A modern audience would probably not take these remarks personally, but hundreds of spectators could have done so in 424 BCE, as tribal representatives on the Council were humorously accused of corruption and allowing the war to drag on. They also were turned into supporters of the meat tradesman, for the price of some garnishes. 'I'm Public Hero Number One,' boasts the sausage vendor, 'Thanks to some coriander and a bunch of leeks' (1993: 93).

To regard the first showing of *The Knights* as an attack on Cleon or just one person's malfeasance is to overlook its teasing of the Council and the Assembly with their thousands of delegates. The playwright was taking on democracy itself, or many of its representatives, questioning their integrity, suggesting Cleon was not the best leader. The humour was not entirely negative, either; he praised the knights, their horses, leeks and coriander. And he rejuvenated Demos. In sessions of the US Congress today, politicians accuse one another of creating 'political theatre', a dismissive term that means they offer a politics of spectacle rather than substance. Aristophanes created another, more substantial kind of political theatre in Athens, as he brought the city-state's legislators into his session, satiric but also constructive as it enacted new, comic changes in government.

Early in the play, a slave points to the audience and asks the sausage seller if he sees the 'rows and rows' of people. He predicts all of them – councillors, generals, police – soon will be led by the newcomer. 'They're yours, all yours. They'll all be under you' (1993: 72–3). The playwright assists the newcomer's rise by writing speeches for him; and the playwright becomes a victor, too, after festival judges award him first prize. After *The Knights*, Aristophanes takes on the government again in plays such as *Lysistrata* (411 BCE), where women capture the Treasury and initiate a sex strike to stop war, and in *The Assembly of Women* (c. 393–391 BCE), where Athenian women disguise themselves as male legislators and pass new laws. Greek theatre director Alexis Solomos argued

that for Aristophanes 'the best way to fight the demagogue of
the Assembly is to become the demagogue of the theatre. After
all, only a few minutes' walk separates the one public platform
from the other' (1974: 90). But the playwright ends their
separation, as he turns his theatre space into a new, enlarged
Assembly, and replaces the reigning demagogue (or his stand-
in) with a reformer.

Shelley called poets unacknowledged legislators. Aristophanes
acknowledged the poets and the legislators, and gave both
groups representatives on his stage. The chorus leader in an
earlier play, *The Acharnians*, asks for honour to be conferred
on poets whose satire prevents orators from misleading the
public; Aristophanes himself wanted to be one of those poets.
In *The Knights* the poet creates a competition for government
leadership and then names the winner. He literally gives the
winner a name. The victor of the Assembly debate in *The
Knights* is first asked his name after he defeats Paphlagon,
and announces he is Agorakritos, which has been translated
as 'chosen by the assembly' (1998: 387) and 'Common Man'
(1993: 120). Aristophanes makes the winner a man of the
people, the assembly's choice, a seasoned debater (seasoned
with coriander and experience). That he is nameless, known
only by his trade until late in the play, suggests a man off the
street, an Everyman, if not any man, would be better than
Cleon, although not every man would be capable of the coarse
language, double-dealing and thievery with which Agorakritos
counters Paphlagon's offences.

Since *The Knights* was the first play for which Aristophanes
sought a chorus under his own name, he resembled Agorakritos
in this respect; he too had withheld his name for a time.
Callistratus had hired a chorus for him previously, perhaps to
protect Aristophanes from reprisals by Cleon. The playwright,
like Agorakritos, was an up-and-coming, not-yet-known
opponent of the city-state's recently victorious general.

Aristophanes has other rivals too, not just Cleon but other
playwrights; although no other complete stage satires from the
period survive, if three comic playwrights competed in each

festival, their collective number produced many comedies from 486 BCE, when comedies first became part of the Dionysian festival, to 388 BCE, when the last surviving play (*Wealth*) by Aristophanes was staged. The names of fifty comic poets from the period are known, according to Henderson, but plays by only one of them remain in print, survivors of an ephemeral art (1996: 4). Was Aristophanes, like Agorakritos, more scrappy and resourceful than his rivals?

Centuries of Invective

Aristophanes's scrappiness can be attributed in part to a facility with invective. Aristophanes has nothing kind to say about Cleon, and he doesn't say it (speaking about Paphlagon instead) with joy and fervour. In other satires he criticizes the Peloponnesian war and regrets its continuation. In *The Knights* he goes to war against a local tyrant. Words are the primary weapon, although some comic physical combat takes place too. Satire itself has been described in military terms through references to the art form's attacks, targets and conquest of enemies. The fact that the battle in *The Knights* is mostly verbal makes it quite appropriate for combat with Cleon. Not a general before he went to Pylos, he was a fierce debater in the Assembly. The tyrant repeatedly called for the death and execution of enemies; Aristophanes mimics this extremism with comic bluster. The changed, more humorous inflection can be sensed by comparing a speech of Cleon's – as reconstructed by Thucydides – to one given by the Athenian leader's stage counterpart. Thucydides records oratory in which Cleon urged Athenians to execute Mytilenian prisoners of war:

> What you do not realize is that your empire is a tyranny exercised over subjects who do not like it and who are always plotting against you; you will not make them obey

you by injuring your own interests in order to do them a favour; your leadership depends on superior strength and not on any goodwill of theirs... Let them now therefore have the punishment which their crime deserves.

(1972: 212–15)

By contrast, Paphlagon offers coarse, short-tempered, comparatively short-winded talk of rebellion and death in *The Knights*, in his first address to two slaves:

By the Twelve Gods, you two won't get away with your unending plots against the people.

What's that Chalcidian cup doing here? It can only mean you're inciting the Chalcidians to revolt! You two are goners, done for, you utter scum! (1998: 261)

The tyrant portrayed here addresses his rivals directly and more abusively than Cleon. Aristophanes makes the demagogue struggle to be meaner than his new opponent. Both characters' parries are usually brief, punchy, inflated with hot air as the combatants ridicule one another repeatedly.

Swift, in his *Battel of the Books*, described a literary war in which much ink was spilled. During performance of *The Knights* words have to be spoken, sung, shouted and growled. Not only the sausage seller but also the chorus directs unflattering phrases at Paphlagon. Their lyrics still sound offensive, although comically so, translated from the Greek by Kenneth McLeish:

Disgusting, loud-mouthed scum!
Muck-peddler! Conman! Bum!
You make everyone sick.
You know every low trick.
You bellow and roar and howl;
You demand
Cash in hand;
You're vile! You stink! You're foul! (1979: 142)

Such pejorative language constitutes an important component of Aristophanic satire, its invective. The spewing of insults at an enemy has origins traced by F. M. Cornford, R. C. Elliott and other scholars to fertility rituals and processions in ancient cultures where curses were recited to expel enemies or evil forces. Aristotle, in his *Poetics*, acknowledges these practices when he refers to 'phallic songs' as the origin of comedy (1961: 57). Reading Aristophanes as if he was still writing phallic songs, some Victorian scholars bowdlerized translations of the plays which they considered obscene. Granted some of his phallic jokes, especially in *Lysistrata*, are crude and archaic in our time. But to see his plays simply as the remnant of a fertility ritual or male exhibitionism requires overlooking the satire Aristophanes directs at promoters of war, peace, religion, law, philosophy and most plays besides his own.

The Frogs, The Knights, The Acharnians, The Clouds, The Birds, The Wasps, The Assembly of Women and *Peace* offer irreverent social commentary on a wide range of issues, as well as small traces of fertility songs and ancient invective. Aristophanes's comic imprecations entertain at the same time they call for a change in attitude towards an adversary. Paphlagon, in *The Knights*, when speaking about his opponent, asks: 'Isn't it awful to hear him say these things about me, Demos, just because I cherish you?' (1998: 331). In fact it is not 'awful' to hear insults thrown at Paphlagon; it could be quite funny, as Cleon's double has to stand and take it, with Cleon himself not far away.

The sausage seller and Paphlagon are well matched. Both have backgrounds in commerce, and their rude speeches employ imagery that might be heard in a marketplace. 'I'll tan your hide,' threatens Paphlagon, whose name connotes a leather merchant's background. The sausage seller threatens to stuff his opponent's guts and mince him up (1993: 82–3). (Centuries later the Russian critic Mikhail Bakhtin would locate another variety of coarse, marketplace language in the satire of Rabelais.) Accusations are also self-directed at times since the least civil, least polite man will be the one to succeed in *The Knights*. The rivals openly admit their efforts to mislead others and advance their position by any means necessary – the more treacherous and cunning, the better.

The world of butchers and street vendors has given Agorakritos skills that make him nastier and more deceptive than his rival. 'Tenderize him, / Pulverize him', the chorus advises their man (1993: 83). Crude, colourful insults objectify men as raw meat, pieces of leather, things to be beaten, crushed, skinned. In translation much of the rude language and primal combat remains accessible to modern spectators, and needs no annotations. MacLeish describes the play as a 'cartoon-like caricature' that 'contains some of Aristophanes' crudest, coarsest jokes, and its political commentary (the most overt in all his works) is rammed home with all the delicacy of Hogarth, Gillray or Gerald Scarfe' (Aristophanes 1979: xii). The art of Hogarth, Gillray and Scarfe was not always delicate, of course; some of their satiric engravings depict riotous and improper social situations. The graphic illustrations came with captions, but not with pages of offensive and comic language. For that we have to turn to Aristophanes and his successors.

Satiric invective surfaces in later periods of theatre, too, particularly in the plays of Ben Jonson, who read Aristophanes. Characters in Act Four, Scene Four of *Bartholomew Fair* (1614) play a game of 'vapours' where rules require disagreement. In the same play, the Puritan Rabbi Busy debates a puppet named Dionysus, briefly returning satire to its ancient origins with the Greek god's name given to one of the arguers, who happens to be a hand puppet at the fair. Leaping ahead three and a half centuries, India's radical theatre artist Utpal Dutt could be heard unleashing invective against his nation's leaders to entertain large *jatra* audiences of 20,000 with 'caricatures, horseplay, mugging, doubletakes, puns, kicks, bumps, and grinds' (Bharucha 1979: 76). In a smaller Paris venue, two tramps onstage for Beckett's *Waiting for Godot* (1953) played a game in which they insulted each other to pass the time, and the worst insult turned out to be the word 'critic'. Their name-calling directed at the theatre world recalls Aristophanes repeatedly directing insults at fellow writers. Euripides, Aeschylus, Phrynichos, Lykis, Ameipsias, all playwrights ancient Athenians would have known, are targets of mockery in *The Frogs*.

Disrespectful language constitutes a major weapon in these satiric contests, but it is not the only one. Verbal insults are often accompanied by physical assaults that repel an intruder, and by gifts or bribes meant to win supporters. In *The Knights* the sausage seller offers Demos a pair of sandals and a tunic to the dismay of his rival. Paphlagon's competing offer of his own jacket is rejected when Demos claims the leather merchant's clothing smells of its origin. This gift-giving sets the stage for talk of corruption and price fixing.

Cleon also may have been mocked physically onstage through a special style of oratory. According to MacDowell, earlier orators 'had kept their hands inside their cloaks, but Kleon evidently slipped his cloak off one or both shoulders, having it secured by a belt, to enable him to gesticulate with his hands so as to hold the attention of the crowd'. Hand gestures contributed to his reputation as a 'violent' orator, 'which probably means shouting and rudeness' were part of his addresses (MacDowell 1995: 82). At one point Aristophanes has Cleon's stand-in boast 'nothing gets plotted in the city that I'm not aware of and immediately screaming about', which confirms his tendency to shout (1998: 335). The leather seller also removes his jacket completely, and gives it to Demos around line 890, which frees his arms more than usual and allows him to flail wildly as he threatens Agorakritos.

In response to this temper-tantrum, the sausage seller notes his opponent is boiling with fury, further suggesting that Paphlagon with his outer garment removed would be a fiery and comically flailing orator. Macleish notes that while Paphlagon's name literally means 'the man from Paphlagonia', it also puns on *paphlasdon*, meaning 'Foaming-at-the-mouth', a clue to the way an actor might speak this character's lines (1979: xii). At the end of the play the defeated orator surrenders his crown to Agorakritos and goes speechless. End of flailing and fury, exit tyrant.

The Timorous Mask Maker

Audience recognition of those impersonated was facilitated by masks showing famous faces in some satires. At the performance of Aristophanes's *The Clouds* (423 BCE), spectators asked Socrates to stand so they could compare the philosopher to the actor mimicking him. It was the opposite of a standing ovation; everyone else probably sat as Socrates rose to be compared to his clownish, masked counterpart. We have no record of Cleon being asked to stand at *The Knights*, but by all accounts he sat in the front row. Ironically, his placement there was due to his alleged victory at Pylos. Rewards for the triumph included front row seating, an honour that facilitated his dishonour.

Because he sat there, actors easily could point Cleon out. Pointing may have been necessary, if thousands of spectators seated in rows behind him could see only see the back of his head. That may have been just as well, since no mask maker dared replicate Cleon's face. The audience had no need to compare the two. Aristophanes may have played the role of Paphlagon himself, unmasked, or portrayed the sausage seller. Solomos speculates either role could have been his (1974: 97–101). *The Knights* includes a self-referential joke about the mask maker's fear of reprisal before Paphlagon appears on stage: 'And never fear, he's not portrayed to the life: none of the mask makers had the guts to make a portrait mask. He'll be recognized all the same, because the audience is smart' (1998: 259).

The critic Halliwell argues it doesn't matter if the face mask was absent or inaccurate in stage impersonations of Socrates, Euripides and Cleon. Aristophanes's procedure as a writer was:

not to focus on particular features or traits, but rather to turn the nominally real individual into an exaggerated and easily recognizable type. The person's identity, and some of his associations, form the basis for a structure of more or less fictional characterization in terms which can be appreciated by a large popular audience, whether or not they have a detailed acquaintance with the particular target.

Halliwell sees reduced moral force and greater comedy rising from this procedure (1984: 10). While modern audiences may readily appreciate the attack on a 'type' of person and find it funnier than references to specific individuals, the importance in 424 BCE of references to a living individual such as Cleon should not be underestimated; the play's first 'smart' audience would have recognized the man in the front row as the target of many jokes, even if they saw only the back of his head. The satire was not directed at a generic thief, bribe giver or impostor but a particular demagogue. Some attributions may be exaggerated or fictitious, and some references may now seem obscure even in the best translations; but at the first performance these jibes at Cleon were more personal and timely than a 'fictional characterization'.

Satire departs far from reality at the conclusion of *The Knights*, as Cleon's double loses the contest and his sway over Demos. Demos acquires a new look (new mask, clothing and brooch mentioned earlier) and peace treaties. In reality, after the play ended war continued and Cleon 'remained in power, and his method and manner of politics hardly changed' (MacLeish 1979: xiii). The hour or two of satire at the Lenaea amounted to a brief usurpation, an upheaval that temporarily changed the government and offered a glimpse of an alternative ruler.

Cleon's continued rule, and the survival of other men satirized in other plays discussed later, might lead a critic to conclude as one did: 'Most satire is, by its very nature, destructive and impractical…. If [the satirist] has any positive social function at all, it is purely purgative; relieving the spectator of his outrage and frustration over the forces which manipulate his fate' (Brustein 1965: 191). From this perspective, any glimpse of an alternative society is simply part of the relief from outrage and frustration. But theatre history renders another verdict. Cleon, like some other prominent men mocked on stage, is now remembered for the role in which a satirist cast him. The satire functions as a corrective over time, if not immediately. A portrait of Cleon offered by Thucydides in his historical record is unflattering, too, but less humorous, and not one that can bring the demagogue back for more pummelling on stage as *The Knights* has. Aristophanes initiated Cleon's future as a comic character, one in a line of political, cultural and fashion leaders scathed by satire. The playwright even forced Cleon to praise his attacker in *The Knights*; his stand-in Paphlagon complains – or boasts – about the humour directed at him: 'see what outrageous insults I'm taking' (1998: 317).

When gifted satirists like Aristophanes find a deserving subject, more than one play may be in order. Aristophanes mocked Cleon in six plays. Judging from the tyrant's responses, rather than finding relief in the plays, he needed relief from them. His 'purgative' was a court of law. Two years before *The Knights*, another play by Aristophanes, *The Babylonians* (426 BCE), now lost, prompted Cleon to initiate legal prosecution for personal attacks. Athenians were reminded about this clash in the *parabasis* of *The Acharnians* (425 BCE), not lost, where Dikaipolis recalls how 'last year's comedy provoked [Cleon] to say the least. He dragged me [meaning Aristophanes] into the Senate House, sued me, and opened the sluicegates. Slander and lies gushed from his tongue' (1969: 33). The ridicule continued a year later in *The Knights*, after which another lawsuit arose and was settled out of court. Even Cleon's death could not win him immunity from Aristophanes's humour. After hearing a report of the general's demise in *Peace* (421 BCE), an Athenian named Trygaios responds: 'Thank god for that. / I always said if you gave Kleon time, / He was bound to do something right' (1993: 142). Cleon's reputation, also attacked in *The Clouds* and *The Wasps*, had become a running gag.

The Secret of Satire Revealed

Disclosure of Cleon's identity as a cheat and overrated war veteran through name-calling, jokes about his deceptive practices and imitation of his oratorical style are a continuing action in *The Knights*. It constitutes an extended recognition scene that differs from those analysed by Aristotle in his *Poetics*. Aristotle's concept of recognition (*anagnorsis*) involves a tragic character's delayed discovery of a blood relative. Oedipus, for example, discovers that he has married his mother. Instead of tragic *anagnorsis* Aristophanes promotes satiric recognition of identities by the audience. The antagonist's resemblance to an off-stage counterpart (i.e. Paphlagon behaves like Cleon, both are scoundrels) is suggested early and often. The intensity of the recognition increases through sustained, repeated delivery of insulting adjectives and aspersions cast at a particular Athenian. Henderson confirms the importance of this specificity in satire when he notes that Aristophanes 'expressed greater pride in *Knights* than in any other of his plays, claiming that it inaugurated a new genre of "demagogue comedy" and boasting of his own personal courage, and success, in attacking the most dangerous of the demagogues' (1998: 223).

Over time, Roman comedy with its romantic intrigue between young lovers became far more popular on stage than the kind of the topical humour Aristophanes offered. Spectator identification with a protagonist is more likely to take place in an Aristotelian tragedy or Roman comedy and their later variations than in satire, which has a different effect. As the plot of romantic comedy builds from one scene to the next, audience members identify with lead characters who overcome parental objections and other interference. Comic obstacles to a couple's marriage generate empathy for the lovers. The legacy of empathic theatre can be seen in Hollywood films and television serials. The hero, who averts tragedy, stops a runaway train or saves a kidnapped heiress, has a romantic comedy counterpart in films where he or she may be chasing a partner instead of a mad bomber; in either situation, spectators are likely to side with the anguished hero or heroine, and find relief in his or her triumph. Satire is almost the opposite; instead of empathy, it promotes a joyful antipathy. If spectators side with the sausage sellers of the world against Paphlagonians, it is because they enjoy the direction of ridicule at a person they recognize, in this instance a blustering miscreant. Humorous attacks on Cleon's stand-in encouraged the audience to look askance at the character and lose any respect they had for his off-stage double.

Athenians must have known in 424 BCE that the rescue of Athens and Demos from a politician's misrule was a fantasy. But even friends of Cleon could have found some affirmation in *The Knights*; for all its negative humour, the play defends democracy and its embodiment, Demos, against abuse. Cleon's stand-in claims he cherishes Demos more than any other citizen; he is boasting again, perhaps, but also paying homage to Athens and its government, as does the playwright who leaves Demos in better condition than he found him. In *The Knights* Aristophanes voices greater respect for past leaders than those in power; but he sees a need for continuing democracy. His play mocks the Assembly, but also convenes it to witness a fierce debate. His longing for past glory in *The Knights*, also in *The Frogs* which pays tribute to Aeschylus's depiction of war heroes and reproaches Euripides for his tarnished heroes, testifies to a preservationist's interests.

Towards the end of *The Frogs*, the god of theatre asks Aeschylus and Euripides, 'How can we save the city?' (1969: 87). There and in *The Acharnians* Aristophanes declares that playwrights should serve Athens, and so his satire does through its comic antipathy towards misconduct at the top, its attacks on selected Greeks. While *The Knights* was written relatively early in his career, its defence of 'the people' (Demos) against a leader Aristophanes finds harmful anticipates his later positions favouring peace treaties and poets who serve the state. During his lifetime Athens was far from perfect with its imperialism, sexism, slavery and losing warfare; but thanks to the imperfections (some of which he overlooked), the playwright was able to serve the city-state by offering satiric correctives. This is not to say that he changed society or its leaders, but he brought thousands of citizens together to see leadership chastised and contested in a new comic Assembly.

Cleon's Other Names

The comic distortions and unruly assaults on his contemporaries that Aristophanes devised now have value as historical documents; they provide a wealth of information about how stage satire once flourished and responded to war and demagoguery as well as democracy. The satirist's assault on Cleon still can be viewed on stage occasionally in adaptations; the ancient Greek tyrant's arrogance has modern counterparts, even if the new malefactors differ in details from the old. Cleon was by no means the last braggart and bully to govern a democratic state. A case could be made in 2020 for staging *The Knights* as a satire of Donald Trump–like politicians. The 45th American President's provocative, aggressive campaigning to make himself and America 'great' has an antecedent in Aristophanes.

Sausage Seller: Tell me, just how does a sausage seller like me become a big shot?

First Slave [Demosthenes]: That's precisely why you're going to be great, because you're loudmouthed, low class and down market.

(1998: 253–5)

According to a *New Yorker* report by James Romma, during the 2016 election campaign in the United States, a Barnard College, New York, production of *The Knights* cast a Donald Trump impersonator as the sausage seller, and presidential contender Hillary Clinton as Cleon. 'The play presents a contest between them as a race to the bottom,' wrote Romma, 'with the Demos, or citizenry, reimagined as a gaggle of female newscasters, anointing Trump as its new champion' (2016). The production showed that 'democratic leadership is always getting worse', according to the article. That is not exactly what Aristophanes thought when he re-costumed Demos at the end of *The Knights* and had the sausage seller cease his base behaviour after winning the contest. But it might be agreed that in the 2016 election, as in *The Knights*, offensive and brazen speeches enabled one candidate to defeat another. As long as politicians continue to speak shamelessly and display tyrannical behaviour, a play like *The Knights* will lend itself to adaptation.

A few modern Greek productions of the play directed satire at contemporary leaders. Gonda A. H. Van Steen reports in *Venom in Verse: Aristophanes in Modern Greece* that a 1974 production of *The Knights* responded to the rise of a junta in Athens, and 'the cast presented a parabasis of its own making, which amounted to an explicit denunciation of the recently abolished dictatorship' (2000: 211). A Greek theatre group at Epidaurus 'presented the *Knights* in 1989, a year when the right-wing New Democracy replaced PASOK [and the populism of Andreas Papandreou] as ruling party'. Van Steen adds that 'a politicized Aristophanes ... absorbs and punctures political rhetoric with remarkable ease' in periods of rivalry (2000: 213–14).

From Aristophanes to
Saturday Night Live

While billionaire Donald Trump is probably too wealthy and too indifferent to democracy (alias Demos) to qualify as a contemporary Cleon, the contrast between his response to satire and that of the Athenian politician mocked in *The*

Knights provides one measure of changes now taking place in satire's reception as well as its targets. Cleon responded to the play with a lawsuit. A 2019 comic television sketch that mocked Trump led him to broadcast electronically (Tweet) threats of retribution against the producers who facilitated his impersonation on *Saturday Night Live*. Trump's complaints about impersonation of him by actor Alec Baldwin called for the Federal Election Commission and Federal Communications Commission to investigate whether such one-sided mockery was fair, since he had no opportunity to respond on the program. 'It's truly incredible that shows like Saturday Night Live, not funny/no talent, can spend all of their time knocking the same person (me), over & over, without so much of a mention of "the other side,"' wrote the President (Deerwester 2019). Baldwin answered by Tweet that Trump was no longer a candidate; as an elected President, he was not entitled to equal time under a fairness doctrine the FCC prescribed for electoral campaigns. No FCC action followed. But Trump himself often attacked opponents through electronic Twitter postings to which his targets had no equally wide-read means of responding; if anyone was unfair, it was the President using his bully pulpit of high office and access to seventy million Twitter accounts to criticize his critics.

Baldwin's 2019 satire of Trump reached a large audience sitting at home in front of TV sets, and continued through other instalments in 2020. But it could be argued that having an audience of 17,000 citizens laughing at Cleon's double in 424 BCE, while the tyrant himself sat in the front row, facilitated more effective satire, particularly if Cleon had any sense of shame. Trump sitting on a White House couch, with no public watching him watch his impersonator, would hear studio laughter from a safe distance. If he had the sense to remain quiet, and not announce his dismay in a public Tweet, the satire might have been forgotten sooner than it was. The good news is that the President's complaint proves satire still can disturb its target and amuse an audience. A leader's ability to defend himself from criticism is at least briefly suspended when satirists and actors take charge of the situation, take their adversary hostage by impersonating him and say whatever they please within Federal Communications Commission guidelines. In these celebratory upheavals, even one lasting only a few minutes, a powerful man can be forced to make concessions, or completely change his policy, although the takeover and change end with the television broadcast.

As for Aristophanes and his plays in our time, if we see *The Knights* in a production that is not an adaptation, the comic acting and underhanded characters still could be entertaining. Classical satire still can provoke laughter through its physical comedy, absurd plots and invective. As the war of insults between two men heats up in *The Knights*, these dirty fighters do not differ so much (except in their colourful vocabulary) from newer politicians capable of bullying, boasting, lying, soliciting favours and winning re-election. Their arena for misbehaviour may be unusual, if it is a stage rather than a campaign rostrum on camera. In any case, the supply of misconduct in the world is far from exhausted; only the number of playwrights presenting satires annually as Aristophanes and others did in Athens seems to be limited.

Wandering Fifteen Hundred Years: Minstrelsy and Popular Theatre

While state-sponsored festivals in Athens paid for plays by Aristophanes and his contemporaries, satires of everyday life were staged without government subsidy by ancient Greek mimes such as Herondas. His one-act 'mimes' employed verbal and physical comedy. Not silent, mime plays featured a series of speaking roles all performed by the same actor. Undated, probably written in the third century BCE, surviving texts by Herondas include one playlet about a shoemaker named Kerdon who encourages female customers to make a purchase. 'We'll keep showing until you're pleased,' he vows, but a woman named Metro proves impossible to satisfy. 'Fits to perfection. What possible improvement could you want?... You would think Athena made this shoe,' the cobbler says; but after showing all his leather wares he ends up with no sale. Guy Davenport, translator of Herondas's *The Shoemaker* and other scenes, imagines the acting of this mime in ancient times was 'close to the art of Peter Sellers, of Zero Mostel, and Lily Tomlin', gifted modern comedians and each 'a master impersonator of types', although he adds that the performances in Greece may have been 'more savagely satiric' (1981: xii). Sue-Ellen Case has speculated that some mime artists could have been women whose names went unrecorded, and whose plays 'included satires on local personalities and current events' (1988: 29).

One-person performances on the streets of Greece constituted a form of popular theatre that continues to this day among artists who tour and ask for audience support after their show. In the past century Dario Fo renewed practices of minstrels and jesters by adapting biblical and medieval tales. One of the Italian satirist's sketches introduces the first Christian troubadour (*jongleur*), who speaks for the poor and the oppressed after Christ blesses him. In Fo's *Birth of the Jongleur* Jesus informs his disciple:

> I have come here to give you the power of speech. And this tongue of yours will lash, and slash like a sword .... You will speak out against bosses, and crush them, so that others can understand and learn, so that others can laugh at them and make fun of them, because it is only with laughter that the bosses will be destroyed.
>
> (Fo 1988: 53)

His series of tales about the Catholic Church, influenced by Fo's own heterodox Marxist perspective on class struggle and collected under the title of *Mistero Buffo*, included a re-enactment of the resurrection of Lazarus in which Fo portrayed a whole crowd of spectators watching the dead

man revive. Scenes in his history of the Church, especially
Fo's impersonation of Popes, won the enmity of the Vatican.
His stories brought back (like Lazarus) the voices of the
underclass, ordinary people from past ages, in scenes imbued
with contemporary humour and class-consciousness. Dario
Fo and his wife, actress and writer Franca Rame, attracted
large receptive audiences for their one-person shows in Italy
and internationally when they toured (Figure 4). One summer
night I watched them entertain thousands in a small town
square in Gubbio, Italy. They stood on a wooden platform
stage assembled for that night only and performed satiric
monologues about church, state and marriage. Like their full-
length plays, the one-person satires drew on popular traditions
of cabaret, Italian fishermen's storytelling, *commedia dell'arte*,
and the practices of Christian jongleurs. Their full-length
satires such as *Throw the Lady Out* (1967), *Accidental Death
of an Anarchist* (1970, discussed later) and *We Can't Pay, We
Won't Pay* (1974) attracted international praise too.

When I met Fo in Gubbio, I asked him about other
contemporary theatre artists who were friendly or rival
satirists. He regretted there were very few. Besides his own
acting company, he found support in, and drew inspiration
from, earlier satirists he discusses in *The Tricks of the Trade*,
a collection of talks. There he referred to *commedia dell'arte*,
Aristophanes, mimes, minstrels and clowns who preceded
him, as well as Brecht and other contemporary theatre artists.
He acknowledged Aristophanes as one of his models when he
wrote: 'It is well known that in the comedies of Aristophanes
a broad clowning routine, including knockabout, a wide
repertory of slaps and punches not to mention an array of the
most obscene jokes, were the order of the day' (Fo 1991: 178).

The writings of Aristophanes were known to other satirists,
notably self-taught Elizabethan Ben Jonson, who caustically
refers to London life and a changing society that is both
Puritanical and acquisitive in plays such as *The Alchemist* and
Bartholomew Fair. Samuel Foote (1720–77) has been called
the English Aristophanes. As actor and author he mimicked

Figure 4 *Dario Fo and Franca Rame, 1985.*

contemporaries on stage, and included some self-satire in *The Author* (1757). Traces of the Aristophanic tradition also can be found in S. J. Perelman's satire of American artists and their patrons in *The Beauty Part*, discussed later.

Ben Jonson after Aristophanes

Writing in a society where new wealth was raised through colonial exploits, trading companies and financial speculation, Jonson (1572–1637) satirized the acquisitive behaviour of his countrymen. In the tradition of Aristophanes's satire *Plutus* (also known as *Wealth*), *Volpone* (1606) deals with society's corruption by avarice. While the play has no chorus of frogs or birds, human characters in *Volpone* are named after the fox, fly, vulture and crow, and they behave as predators, although monetary wealth, rather than food, is the reward for which they prey. (The ultimate performance of Aesopian satire was developed three centuries later by a Russian circus clown, Vladimir Durov, who trained pigs to handle money, pistols and other human props. For more see Schechter 1985.) Setting *Volpone* in Italy, Jonson was able to portray vicious financial schemes and commodity fetishism without having to worry that he would be accused of maligning England. That concern did not deter him from locating other satires in London.

Elizabethan England fostered a new merchant class and a theatre that was mercantile, too, insofar as it collected admission fees to pay its artists. Jonson never earned great sums from his satires; his masques for the court of King James brought him more income, although they are now staged and read far less frequently than *Volpone, The Alchemist* (1610) and *Bartholomew Fair* (1614). The latter two works portrayed life in London with all its hypocrisy, cunning, folly, appetite and concupiscence, as Shakespeare did not. The creator of Falstaff, Malvolio and Rosalind preferred to recreate English life from earlier times, or set his characters in foreign lands, in history plays and comedies lacking the contemporary settings and local references Jonson incorporated into his finest stage satire. Director Joan Littlewood, who staged a number of Jonson's satires to acclaim in Stratford East, England, in the mid-twentieth century, once defended her preference for his plays in a Theatre Workshop manifesto by declaring: 'We want a theatre with a living language, a theatre which is not afraid of the sound of its own voice and which will comment as fearlessly on Society as did Ben Jonson and Aristophanes' (1979: 161).

While Joan Littlewood directed some audacious new stage satires that will be considered later, as well as plays by Jonson and Aristophanes, the early history of satire is not filled with the names of women. Male actors portrayed females on stage in ancient Greece and Elizabethan England, as well as Japan and China for centuries, and women are not credited with writing plays until the tenth century CE. One could argue that women had a voice in satire early in its history – but it was the voice men gave their characters. The first woman known to write plays in Western theatre was the canoness Hrotsvitha of Gandersheim (935–973 CE). Her tenth-century scripts were based in part on the Roman comedies of Terence. Although not usually celebrated for its satire, Hrotsvitha's play *Dulcitius* mocks patriarchy and empire, as Romans and their disbelief in Christ are found wanting. Roman Governor Dulcitius visits Christian virgins to 'enjoy their embraces' and ends up blackened by the soot of kitchen utensils that prevent his assault on maidens. 'Look, the foolish fellow must be out of his mind; he thinks he is embracing us... Now he hugs the kettle, now the frying pans, and now he hugs the pots, caressing them with soft kisses,' observes Irena, who later welcomes death as a martyr (Gassner 1963: 6). Sue-Ellen Case sees this scene as a 'witty comment on the confusion of male desire', wherein 'Dulcitius cannot distinguish women from the tools of their trade' (1988: 33).

Later some of the first women writing for English theatre satirized gender roles, marriage and patriarchal authority in plays such as Aphra Behn's *The Rover* (1677) and Hannah Cowley's *The Belle's Stratagem* (1780). Cowley's critique of conventional marriage and courtship can be heard in the belle Letitia's description of a bachelor named Doricourt: 'A husband of fifteen months could not have examined me with more cutting indifference.' Plays written and performed by women during the Long Eighteenth Century deserve attention, notably those by Aphra Behn, Suzanne Centlivre, Hannah Cowley, Charlotte Charke and Kitty Clive, all of whom placed new female characters on stage and saw actresses perform the roles. But the woman associated with the eighteenth-century's most popular English satire was created by a man. Polly Peachum, first introduced in *The Beggar's Opera* and featured in a sequel titled *Polly*, was idolized by London theatregoers. Actresses competed for her role, and authors claiming to be Polly Peachum published pamphlets under her name. Curiously, her creator, playwright John Gay, kept his own name out of the ballad opera that introduced Miss Peachum to the world. His satire begins by attributing the play's authorship to a nameless beggar.

3

John Gay's Swiftian Satire in the Long Eighteenth Century

I but transcribe; for not a line
Of all the satire shall be mine.

– SWIFT, 'THE JOURNAL OF A MODERN LADY' (1754: 229)

The denial of authorship, the preference for a pseudonym such as Beggar or Lemuel Gulliver or M. B. Drapier (the last two employed by Jonathan Swift), was sometimes necessary to protect a writer from prosecution in the eighteenth century, an age when Swift, John Gay and Henry Fielding found themselves facing state censorship and arrest for their satire. Each of them created alternate authorial personae – other men to take credit as well as blame for their writing. Gay and Fielding placed in their plays characters who said they wrote the work. Playwrights named Luckless, Trapwit, Fustian, Medley and Spatter appear as authors in Fielding's satires and introduce scenes they claim to have written in *The Author's Farce* (1730), *Pasquin* (1736), *The Historical Register for the Year 1736* (1737) and *Eurydyce Hiss'd* (1737). The humour is self-reflective as it comments on the state of theatre, also slightly self-protective, as Fielding and Gay (alias Beggar) attribute to others faults in government and new playwriting.

At the beginning of *The Beggar's Opera* (1728), the character known only as Beggar claims he wrote 'this Piece' for a marriage celebration. His career as an impoverished poet and mendicant is not entirely different from John Gay's. Gay often depended on support from friends and he wanted – if not begged for – a government sinecure to subsidize his writing. Most of *The Beggar's Opera* portrays other characters – thieves, officers of the law, prostitutes – but the alleged author of the piece returns before it ends to help conclude it. When attributing the author's role to the Beggar, Gay might have joined his friend Swift in contending 'not a line / Of all the satire shall be mine'.

Audiences attending the play when it opened on 29 January 1728 also probably thought at first that the lives of the beggars and highwaymen on stage were far removed from their own; the first scene is set in a den of thieves. But the satire that followed might have surprised and threatened spectators, as it contended that London's lower class and criminal elements were not so different from persons of wealth and fashion. 'Through the whole Piece you may observe such a similitude of manner in high and low Life', the author/Beggar informs us late in the play, 'that it is difficult to determine whether (in the fashionable Vices) the fine Gentlemen imitate the Gentlemen of the Road, or the Gentlemen of the Road the fine Gentlemen' (Gay 2013: 69). Not only 'fine Gentlemen' but also lawyers, courtiers, tradesmen, fine ladies, others who had counterparts in the audience received dishonourable mention in the play.

The play's presentation of thieves and beggars was artful, witty, by no means a simple transfer of London street life onto the stage. Although the lives of famous criminals gave Gay inspiration for some roles, his characters often spoke with wit and sang rhymed lyrics, not the usual expressions of eighteenth-century Londoners who earned a living as highway robbers, pickpockets and whores. This new kind of play known as a 'ballad opera' also offered the audience dialogue and songs in English at a time when Italian opera was in vogue. Suddenly spectators were able to understand the words, including comic and romantic lyrics sung to familiar folk tunes. Foreign language opera was not only mocked but overtaken in popularity by Gay's play. Not content with seeing his characters on stage, townspeople brought them home – decorated their dwellings with fans, fire screens and playing cards bearing images of Polly Peachum and her husband, the highwayman Macheath.

Unlike Athenian satires staged once for an audience of 17,000, *The Beggar's Opera* was repeated as long as audiences were willing to pay for it. Lincoln's Inn Fields seated 1,400 people; since the play ran sixty-two nights in its first season, 86,800 spectators could have watched Gay's satire during that period. Ironically, the opera with origins attributed to a beggar and his impoverished theatre group became a source of wealth for Gay and his theatre's manager, John Rich. *The Beggar's Opera* was said to have made Gay rich and Rich gay. By 20 March 1728, less than two months after the play opened, Gay was able to inform his friend Swift: 'I have got by all this success, between seven and eight hundred pounds, and Rich... hath cleared already near four thousand pounds' (Gay 1973: xvii). Swift, as one satirist supportive of another, replied to Gay on 28 March 1728: 'I think that rich rogue Rich Should in conscience make you a present of 2 or 3 hundred Guineas. I am impatient that such a dog by Sitting Still Should get five times more than the Author.'

Gay had no complaints; in fact, he wrote another play, a sequel, for Rich to stage. Together they had found a new way to make money from begging. Londoners eagerly paid to see well-spoken rogues, prostitutes and thieves sing. Ticket collection at the door and indoor seating reduced the chance that actual beggars off the street would accost viewers during a performance. Although some sex workers and pickpockets might have paid an entrance fee and pursued their trade inside Lincoln's Inn Fields, most playgoers came from other ways of life that Gay mocked. A few were offended; references to politicians disturbed some leading citizens, as will be seen.

Opposition to the play as well as adulation of it by most spectators helped ensure *The Beggar's Opera*'s notable standing in the history of stage satire.

The play also made its lead actress famous. Women performed roles on the previously all-male English stage after the restoration of King Charles (who loved actresses on- and offstage) in 1660. By 1728, roles for women were not a novelty; but Polly Peachum as portrayed by actress Lavinia Fenton became a great attraction. Gay wrote a sequel titled *Polly* to capitalize on the popularity of both *The Beggar's Opera* and the female character audiences adored. Miss Fenton could have been cast in the sequel, had she not withdrawn from her theatre career to live as the mistress of the Duke of Bolton, who first saw her on stage. A painting by Hogarth commemorates the Duke's love at first sight. Hogarth's canvas (painted and sold in several versions) and an engraving by William Blake of the same scene show the Duke holding a copy of the play text in his hand; but he stares at Fenton, not the book (Figure 5). He and other audience members seated on both sides of the stage are so close to the actors they might be mistaken for visitors at Newgate prison, where the scene is set. The guests on stage include Sir Conyers D'Arcy, producer John Rich, Lady Jane Cook, Sir Robert Fagg, Sir Theodore Robinson and Lord Gage. In Act Three, when the Player speaks of complying with 'the taste of the town', he might have gestured towards spectators beside him, whose applause and laughter would be watched and possibly copied by others in the house.

Speaking of copying, the success of Gay's first ballad opera gave rise to many other new plays with songs in English; most of them, except for Henry Fielding's, were less accomplished and less remunerative than the first. One widely seen, internationally popular sequel to *The Beggar's Opera* took the stage 200 years later when Bertolt Brecht's *Threepenny Opera* opened in Berlin. His 1928 satire reutilized John Gay's characters and some of the original story, although Brecht changed the play to an extent that the German text can be called his own (based on his collaborator Elisabeth Hauptmann's translation). It also

Figure 5 The Beggar's Opera, *Act Three, Scene Eleven, William Blake engraving after Hogarth.*

was distinguished by Kurt Weill's new music. Other rewritings of Gay's play and Brecht's followed. The proliferation of variations on *The Beggar's Opera* demonstrates how stage satire can be renewed; particularly through Brecht's rewriting (discussed in detail later) the lives of the characters born in 1728 were considerably lengthened. Historians usually say the 'Long Eighteenth Century' started with the restoration of monarchy in 1660 and lasted to 1815 or even 1830, but Brecht and other authors who adapted Gay's text extended the duration of the century's popular stage characters several hundred years. At the same time, *The Beggar's Opera* has remained unique to the eighteenth century due to Gay's use of period language and the specific targets chosen for his satire. The jargon of thieves, whores and tradesmen makes some speeches written in 1728 sound arcane today, almost like a lost language. The dialogue is no more difficult to follow than Shakespeare's Elizabethan English, which audiences continue to welcome; but Gay's language has the sound of a particular time and place – that place being the stage rather than the taverns or the highways of Georgian England. Speeches and songs in *The Beggar's Opera* offer heightened, vivid expressions, carefully crafted witticisms. No highwayman except Macheath would sing such beautifully rhymed lyrics to his beloved:

> Were I laid on Greenland's Coast,
> And in my Arms embrac'd my Lass;
> Warm admidst eternal Frost,
> Too soon the Half Year's Night would pass...
> And I would love you all the Day,...
> If with me you'd fondly stray.

These lyrics (Air 16) have the charm and the exaggerated boast one expects from a ballad opera's most wanted man (no ordinary highway robber), who has several wives and even admits that he strays. Polly Peachum's reply in devotional and idyllic lyrics would qualify her as a poetess, if we did not know Gay wrote the lines for this daughter of a dealer in stolen property. Over the centuries these songs have been performed by professional opera singers; a recording session directed by Sir Malcolm Sargent on 10 May 1955, for example, offers the ballads in sonorous renditions that rival the finest traditional opera arias executed in any language by highly trained artists. However, the songs are brief and the dialogue spoken between them can go on at length; we are far from the recitatives and extended arias of Italian opera.

A Satirist at the Opera

Gay's satire let a sizable English-speaking audience understand lyrics as Italian operas had not. According to Roger Fiske there 'was never in England a widespread enthusiasm for Italian opera... it affected only a coterie of society people and intellectuals; the middle and lower class theatergoer inevitably preferred the playhouses where he could understand the words' (1975: 51). Calling itself an opera, the new work lowered or at least changed the standing of opera as a high art by letting a beggar present it. Gay's offering simultaneously mocked aficionados and offered a new, alternative form of theatre featuring commoners and criminals as balladeers. The author and his arranger, Johann Pepusch, drew on tunes many English spectators already knew from folk ballads. Eric Kurtz argues that Gay's 1728 innovations are 'not so much an attack on Italian absurdities' as they are 'an independent reassertion of a native tradition of musical drama' that Henry Purcell pioneered with pastoral and mock-pastoral components in his masque *The Fairy Queen* (1975: 52). Writing new lyrics for pre-existing folk songs and theatre tunes, also continuing Purcell's innovations in mock-pastoral, Gay gave his play's characters 'airs' in several senses of the word: their songs were musical recitals, also conceits, little sermons frequently ironic in outlook. By modern standards, some of the lyrics might be regarded as misogynistic ('Man may escape from Rope and Gun... Who takes a woman must be undone') and misanthropic ('If we [women] grow fond they [men] shun us... leave us when they've won us'). But these references to conquest and betrayal hardly endorse the practices. The integrity of the characters singing is questionable, as most Newgate district habitués except Miss Peachum betray and mislead one another between songs. In Air 44 Macheath sings that 'a true Friend can hardly be met', and he should know. In his part of the world friendship is only a loan men and women 'let out for what they can get'; self-interest and financial interests take priority. Such musical admonitions are offset by other more cheerful lyrics that celebrate love and merrymaking. The last song in the play concludes with comic optimism: 'But think of this Maxim, and put off your Sorrow, / The Wretch of To-day, may be happy To-morrow.'

Gay's satire through song also had distant antecedents in Aristophanes. Although no scores survive for the music played to accompany the chorus in *The Knights* or *The Frogs*, we know there was singing in those ancient Greek plays. (American composer Stephen Sondheim wrote a new score and new lyrics for *The Frogs,* but it did not fare well on Broadway in 2004.) Gay's music was preserved, fortunately, and still can be performed; but over time it may have lost an element of surprise his audience would have experienced. The score reused a number of popular tunes, so spectators in 1728 heard familiar music with new words humorously addressing misbehaviour. The kind of 'recognition scene' mentioned earlier (in Chapter 2) as a component of satiric dialogue is offered through song, too. Hearing Air 7, based on 'Oh London is a fine Town', audiences at *The Beggar's Opera* would have noticed that a tune previously accompanying lyrics about whores in London's 'Fine Town' accompanied Mrs Peachum's words about her daughter: 'Our Polly is a sad Slut! Nor heeds what we have taught her. / I wonder any Man alive will ever rear a daughter.' Like most other songs in the play, this one's source was not Italian or French opera, but English balladry; and the situation addressed concerns characters who would have been recognizable in 1728 as Newgate prison visitors, ne'er-do-wells, neighbours. Audiences walking or driven to Lincoln's Inn Fields to see the play probably passed a few 'sad sluts', beggars and future convicts on the street; in that sense too the opera offered them 'recognition' scenes, with musical accompaniment.

The satire briefly parodied a feud between two of England's Italian opera singers, Bordoni and Cuzzoni, by having Lucy and Polly sing about their rivalry over Macheath. Except for this in-joke, Gay's audiences needed no prior knowledge of foreign opera to appreciate his songs. Earlier he had collaborated with Handel on an opera, *Acis and Galatea* (1718), drawing its mythological lovers from Ovid. Writing the libretto for Handel in English might have helped Gay prepare to write his later, more famous, libretto. Brecht once declared *The Beggar's Opera* was 'a parody of Handel, and it is said to have had a splendid result in that Handel's theatre became ruined' (Brecht 1979: 90). If so, Handel's collaborator contributed to his ruin. Leaving the nymphs and shepherds of *Acis and Galatea* behind, moving on to reprobates living in Newgate's prison district, Gay wrote what has been called a 'mock pastoral'. Mockery turned out to be his *forte*. Instead of a mythical green world, he portrayed London's underworld and its idylls. After facing Polyphemus, the ancient monster in the libretto for Handel, he found other dangerous characters closer to home.

A General Huzza

A few lines in *The Beggar's Opera* encouraged its Georgian audiences to see the highwayman Macheath as a stand-in for England's first Minister. Robert Walpole, like Macheath, was known to have mistresses and lead a gang, although his followers in Parliament profited from patronage rather than armed robbery. Ministerial traits also are attributed to Jeremiah Peachum, fence of stolen goods. Early in the play Mr Peachum admits to a resemblance between a great man like the Minister and himself: 'our employment may be reckoned dishonest, because, like Great Statesmen, we encourage those who betray their Friends'. This line also links Peachum to Jonathan Wild, a notorious criminal who dealt in stolen luxuries and 'peached' on some of his suppliers by betraying them to the law.

Strictly speaking, Walpole was neither a highwayman nor a fence; but Gay's references to bribery and vice led his entire opening night audience to look at the first Minister seated in a box. Supporters of Walpole acknowledged the bite of this moment and others; they took offence and said so in print. In reprisal, performance of Gay's sequel, *Polly*, was banned. Perhaps the Prime Minister would have stopped performance of *The Beggar's Opera* too, had he not been drawn into it and encored lyrics on opening night, a scene witnessed and recounted by actor Charles Macklin. The byplay between the players and the Minister in his stage-box reveals satire at its finest, as lyrics about corruption tempt the Minister to show his resilience, and he does so with a cry of 'encore'. But he was not as enthusiastic as spectators might have thought. According to the *Memoirs of Charles Macklin*, during the play's first night in January 1728:

In the scene where Peachum and Lockit are described settling their accounts, Lockit sings the song:

'When you censure the age, etc.'

Which had such an effect on the audience, that, as if by instinct, the greater part of them threw their eyes on the stage-box, where the Minister was sitting, and loudly encored it. Sir Robert saw the stroke instantly, and saw it with good humour and discretion: for no sooner was the song finished, than he encored it a second time himself, joined in the general applause, and by this means brought the audience into so much good humour with him, that they gave him a general huzza from all parts of the house. (Guerinot and Jilg 1976: 94)

[The complete lyrics to Air 30 read:
   When you censure the Age,
   Be cautious and sage,
   Lest the Courtiers offended should be:
   If you mention Vice or Bribe,
   'Tis so pat to all the Tribe;
   Each crys – that was levell'd at me.]

The Minister initially seemed to welcome the lyrics that censured vice and bribery, and the audience cheered his performance. However, the same account of Walpole's visit adds that 'every night, and for many years afterwards, that The Beggar's Opera was brought out, Macklin used to say, the Minister (Sir Robert Walpole) never could with any satisfaction be present at its representation, on account of the many allusions which the audience thought referred to his character. The first song was thought to point to him – the name of Bob Booty whenever it was mentioned, again raised the laugh against him'.

That laughter continued for years, as the play thrived in London and other cities. Its continuation may have disturbed Walpole more than the opening night, as Macklin's account suggests. After the play opened in Dublin, Swift reported to Gay that 'The Beggars Opera hath knokt down Gulliver', yielding first place in satire to his friend. Its continued performance marked a notable change in stage satire's production apparatus. Unlike the plays of Aristophanes, performed only once outdoors in a state-sponsored festival, Gay's play kept running inside a privately owned theatre as long as audiences would support it. Less than a decade after the 1720 financial scandal known as the 'South Sea Bubble', in which stockholders, including Gay, lost considerable sums, this play with its portrayal of highwaymen and whores proved to be a sound investment. In fact, both of Gay's 'Polly' plays generated high returns. Although stage performance of *Polly* was banned, the author was permitted to publish its text, and book sales brought in far more money (£1,200) than most plays on stage were paying. (Today a first edition of the banned play costs several hundred pounds; in that regard if no other, *Polly* remains a valuable satire.) In the success of these plays the Minister accustomed to having people pay him, or at least accept his patronage in return for their favours, saw the public funding his opposition.

While Gay's satire disturbed Walpole, it hardly unseated him. After King George I died in June 1727, the first Minister retained power and increased his sway over the new monarch through friendship with Queen Caroline. Despite some opposition and public protests, he stayed in office until 1742.

How to Ridicule a Minister

One notable accomplishment of *The Beggar's Opera* is that it
did not have to name Walpole, or have him represented by a
single stand-in; mentions of his nicknames and talk of great
statesmen prompted spectators to see connections between the
Minister and the characters on stage. A critic pseudonymously
signing his play review under the name Caleb Danvers
suggested that jailer Lockit, fence Peachum and highwayman
Macheath each displayed aspects of the first Minister's
unindicted venality and corruption. Raising questions about
the character of the government, as well as the play's criminals
in *The Craftsman* of 17 February 1728, Danvers published
'A Key to the Beggar's Opera' 'to prove, beyond all dispute,
that the Beggar's Opera is the most venomous allegorical libel
against the G_____t [Government] that hath appeared for
many years past. There are some persons who esteem Lockit,
the Keeper, or prime Minister of Newgate, to be the Hero of
the Piece'. The same interpreter argues that Captain Macheath
is 'a Great Man' like Walpole, and 'drawn to asperse somebody
in authority' (Guerinot and Jilg 1976: 88–9).

Since *The Craftsman* was an opposition paper often critical
of Walpole, the Danvers assessment of Gay's ballad opera
may well have been a satire itself. Its ostensible condemnation
of the play's 'libel' amplifies and pays tribute to the satire's
attacks on Walpole. The technique through which characters
in Gay's satire were 'drawn to asperse somebody in authority'
and mock a 'Great Man' involves substitution of nicknames
and pseudonyms for actual names, low-level crimes for acts
of state. A Poet, Gay's spokesperson in the prologue to *Polly*,
argues, 'nobody can overdo it [satire] when he attacks the vice
and not the person'. And the person is not attacked by name,
at least not by his own name if his name is Walpole, in *Polly*
and *The Beggar's Opera*.

In Act One of *The Beggar's Opera*, Mrs Peachum interrupts
her husband's reading of account books after he names one of
his clients: 'Robin of Bagshot, alias Gorgon, alias Bluff Bob,

alias Carbuncle, alias Bob Booty.' She defends 'Bob Booty' as
one of her favourite customers. Mr Peachum says Booty spends
his money on women. These slurs would have been recognized
by many spectators in 1728 as references to Walpole, whose
opponents considered him to be a robber (hence Robin),
and a criminal who might hang out with other highwaymen
at Bagshot Heath (hence Robin of Bagshot). He also was
known to deceive (bluff) listeners and collect loot (booty)
through bribes and gifts. 'Carbuncle' could refer to a blemish
contracted through venereal disease, or simply an ugly face. In
these coded phrases and others an audience ready to welcome
oppositional satire in 1728 would find ample suggestions,
though no direct, factual accusations, of ministerial corruption
and philandering. Different in many ways from the allegory
Aristophanes offered in *The Knights*, with its stand-in for
the tyrant Cleon, Gay's satire also allowed spectators to infer
the name and offences of a wrongdoer who happened to be the
nation's most powerful politician.

Gay explains his technique of writing satire without
naming names, by having two men discuss it in the prologue
to *Polly*:

> **Poet:**... I aim at no particular persons; my strokes are at
> vice in general: but if any men particularly vicious are
> hurt, I make no apology, but leave them to the cure of their
> flatterers .....

> **First Player:** Though your Satryr, Sir, is on vices in general,
> it must and will give offence; every vicious man thinks you
> particular, for conscience will make-self-application.

The same philosophy of 'self-application' surfaces in the
famous lyric (Air 30) Walpole encored, where 'Each crys – That
was levell'd at me'. Of course not everyone cried that phrase.
Some Walpole defenders chose instead to see the play as a
celebration of highway robbery and debauchery. Its references
to political life were overlooked by Dr Thomas Herring, whose

sermon at Lincoln's Inn Chapel condemned Gay's play for its immorality in March 1728.

Although this sermon by the King's Chaplain has been lost, its content was summarized by the chaplain's editor, William Duncombe. The speech commended legislative regulation of entertainments by those 'who were sensible how great an Influence Plays and other Diversions have on the Minds of the Populace', and condemned a play that would 'bring upon the Stage, as a proper Subject for Laughter and Merriment, a Gang of Highwaymen and Pickpockets triumphing in their successful Villainie'. The Chaplain thought: 'The Agreeableness of the Entertainment, and its being adapted to the Taste of the Vulgar, and set to easy Tunes (which almost every-body can remember), makes the Contagion spread wider, and the Consequence the more to be dreaded' (Guerinot and Jilg 1976: 121–4). Herring was the court chaplain to whom Jonathan Swift responded by writing that Gay's play 'will probably do more Good than a thousand Sermons of so stupid, so injudicious and so prostitute a Divine' (Swift 1730: 27). Presumably Herring prostituted his services to Walpole and his followers, although Swift never names them. John Gay also responded to his pulpit critic, Herring, without naming him. In the prologue to *Polly* he has the Poet defend satire by saying: 'The Stage, Sir, hath the privilege of the pulpit to attack vice however dignified or distinguish'd.'

Swift's response to Herring was first published in a Dublin journal, *The Intelligencer*, on 25 May 1728. It is one of the best contemporary assessments of Gay's play, also a succinct discourse on the art of satire. 'A Vindication of Mr. Gay and *The Beggar's Opera*' (briefly quoted in the first chapter) praises the play's 'Humour' and then describes 'this Endowment' as:

the best Ingredient towards that Kind of Satyr, which is most useful, and gives the least Offence; which instead of lashing, laughs Men out of their Follies and Vices, and is the Character which gives Horace the preference to Juvenal. And although some Things are too serious, solemn, or sacred to be turned into Ridicule, yet the Abuses of them are certainly not, since it is allowed that Corruption in Religion, Politics, and Law, may be proper Topics for this Kind of Satyr.

In his 'Vindication' Swift also praises Gay:

... as Author of the Beggar's Opera, wherein he hath by a Turn of Humour, entirely New, placed Vices of all Kinds in the strongest and most odious Light; and thereby done eminent Service, both to Religion and Morality. This appears from the unparallell'd Success he hath met with. All Ranks, Parties and Denominations of Men either crowding to see his Opera, or reading it with Delight in their Closets, even Ministers of State, whom he is thought to have most offended (next to those whom the Actors more immediately represent) appearing frequently at the Theatre, from a Consciousness of their own Innocence, and to convince the World how unjust a Parallel, Malice, Envy, and Disaffection to Government have made.

That a Minister of State would go to the theatre 'frequently' to protest his innocence is doubtful, more likely an ironic reference by Swift to Walpole's one-night stand at the opera. In a private letter to Gay dated 16 February 1728, Swift expressed uncertainty and hope that the play had offended England's corrupt leader: 'Does Walpole think you intended an affront to him in your opera? Pray God he may, for he has held the longest hand at hazard that ever fell to any sharper's share, and keeps his run when the dice are charged.'

Besides writing about the play after it opened, Swift contributed to its inception years earlier by calling for a 'Newgate pastoral'. In retrospect Swift's idea has been given too much credit for the resulting play. Gay achieves far more than Swift's phrase allows, although the self-proclaimed independence of the play's outlaws situates them in a curiously idyllic world analysed by William Empson in his essay 'The Beggar's Opera: Mock Pastoral as the Cult of Independence'. Newgate prison's criminal underworld finds some respite from urban strife in song and fellowship, in tavern comradery, even in jail cell visits by a number of women, scenes that might be considered mock-pastoral. Examining mock-pastoral and mock-heroic motifs in the play, Empson describes an exceptional scene where Mr Peachum 'shows a fleeting sympathy with romantic love', and, as a result, says Empson, 'Swift is beaten clean off the field here,' which is to say, the play is more than a Newgate pastoral, it becomes seriously pastoral at one point (1975: 28).

It is tempting to add that Swift is beaten clean off the field of theatre by Gay. While the Dean of St. Patrick's published scathing and enormously influential pamphlets ridiculing English politics, religion, and colonial rule of Ireland, John Gay was the age's Swift as far as theatrical satire went. Although a great satirist, Swift was no playwright. Dialogues he published as *Genteel and Ingenious Conversations* were adapted for the stage by James Miller in 1740 and lasted one night on a double bill with Shakespeare's *Merry Wives of Windsor*. The participation of popular comedians Henry Woodward and Kitty Clive in the cast could not save it. Another evening of Swift adapted for the stage came from the great English clown Joseph Grimaldi, who turned scenes from *Gulliver's Travels* into a pantomime titled *Harlequin Gulliver*. The 1818 pantomime was one of Grimaldi's most popular shows. But *The Beggar's Opera*, not Miller's or Grimaldi's version of Swift, was the most influential stage satire of the Long Eighteenth Century, if judged by its many imitators and adaptors, as well as its continued performance.

Gay was not a one-play satirist, either. Some of his other writing for the stage might benefit from new production and adaptation; inventively adapted, one of them might become the next *Threepenny Opera*. Before creating *The Beggar's Opera* and *Polly*, Gay wrote *The Mohawks* (1712), *The What D'Ye Call It* (1715) and *Three Hours After Marriage* (1717, co-authored with Pope and Arbuthnot). Later he wrote *Achilles* (another ballad opera, posthumously performed in 1733) and *The Rehearsal at Goatham* (not printed or staged in his lifetime).

A Digression on Parody

While Gay's best plays employ a three-act structure that was conventional for the theatre of his day, he also parodied theatre conventions and invented new hybrid forms. *The Beggar's Opera* was one of those hybrids, but earlier, as if clearing the ground for the new genre of ballad opera, he mocked old genres in the title, subtitle and actions of *The Mohocks, A Tragi-Comical Farce* and *The What D'Ye Call It, a Tragi-Comi-Pastoral Farce*. First Aristophanes, later Gay and Fielding engaged in theatrical parody that could be considered a subcategory of satire. Gay in *The What D'Ye Call It* and Fielding in his *Tragedy of Tragedies* (1731) ridicule earlier English theatre by incorporating exaggerations of naïve and pretentious speech, and caricaturing sentimental tragedy to make it more absurd than they found it. Their parodic play titles recall the playlet Shakespeare's rude mechanicals rehearsed – 'The most lamentable comedy and most cruel death of Pyramus and Thisby' – 'very tragical mirth' in *A Midsummer Night's Dream*. Shakespeare too parodied unsophisticated acting and playwriting that preceded his company's efforts.

Placing a rustic, mock-tragic play-within-a-play in *The What D'Ye Call It*, Gay has Kitty, the steward's daughter, tell her beloved Filbert: 'To part is death.' ''Tis death to part'. Filbert woefully replies because he has been pressed into war (1969: 88). Like Macheath thirteen years later, Filbert is granted a reprieve, tragedy is averted and the play's commissioner, Sir Roger, who asked for 'a Tragedy and a Comedy… a Pastoral too', with ghosts, receives all that plus a new daughter-in-law before Gay's parody ends.

Earlier, beginning in 1713 Gay gained experience in parody, satire and collaborative creation when he joined Swift, Alexander Pope, Thomas Parnell and John Arbuthnaut, all members of the Scriblerus Club dedicated to an imaginary pedant named Martinus Scriblerus. (Fielding assigned authorship of his parodic *Tragedy of Tragedies* to H. Scriblerus

Secondus in 1731, and retroactively joined the group.) By co-creating the life and work of Scriblerus, Swift, Gay and friends might be said to have formed their own theatre company; they all played the role of Scriblerus, and 'spoke' in his voice by co-writing his memoirs. When the critic Richardo Quintana says that 'Swift's method is uniformly by way of dramatic satire', and 'his characters are in complete charge', he might also be writing about the Scriblerians as a group (1964: 92). Co-creating the life of Scriblerus, joining with Swift and Pope to compose the ballad *Molly Mog* (1726), and with Pope and Arbuthnot to pen *Three Hours after Marriage*, Gay let the fictitious characters take charge, gave up his own identity or joined it with others. By 1728, he was ready to give a beggar credit for authorship of *The Beggar's Opera*.

When the Scriblerians first formed their group, they may not have been worried about censorship or arrest, and had less need to employ a pseudonym. They enjoyed the privilege of friendship with government officials during the reign of Queen Anne. Swift was commissioned to write pamphlets for the Tories. After the Queen's death in 1714 and the ascension of Whig leaders during the reign of King George, the Scriblerians fell out of favour and their satire turned against leading politicians, particularly Walpole as he consolidated his power. Swift had several close calls with the law after anonymously publishing pamphlets, for one of which his printer was arrested in 1720. The greatest satiric travelogue of the eighteenth century, *Gulliver's Travels*, was published under Lemuel Gulliver's name, and the Dean of St. Patrick's took care to submit the manuscript to a publisher without his own identity being detected.

Gay Declines to Usher Princess Louisa

Theatre production was regulated, too, during John Gay's theatre career. Royal license was granted only to two stages: Lincoln's Inn Fields and Drury Lane. Other smaller, unlicensed theatres opened, among them the Little Theatre in the Haymarket where Henry Fielding directed his own plays in the 1730s. But Fielding's career as a satirist came to an end in May 1737. He was planning to open a version of *Polly* at the time. A new Licensing Act passed later that year might have stopped the staging of his *Macheath Turn'd Pyrate; or, Polly in India*, had the Little Theatre's owner not closed the place first, anticipating a government shutdown. Fielding subsequently left the theatre, became a Justice of the Peace and began writing novels, but not before he ridiculed Walpole in *The Historical Register for the Year 1736,* around the same time he was adapting *Polly.* Written before the shutdown of his theatre, one eerily prophetic scene in *The Historical Register* has a playwright named Medley asked, 'What's become of your two *Pollys*?' and he answers, 'Damn'd, Sir... they were damn'd at my first Rehearsal.' The line refers to rival actresses seeking Polly's role in London; but it also suggests Miss Peachum's life on stage was troubled, and anticipated the cancellation of *Polly in India*, the second of two *Pollys*.

Before *The Beggar's Opera* opened, John Gay's disaffection with Walpole was muted. He served as Commissioner of the State Lottery from 1723 to 1731, and was paid £150 annually for that position; but he had hopes for greater financial support through a preferment. The decisive event in his disillusionment with such prospects arose in October 1727, when Gay was offered the privilege of serving as Gentleman Usher to Princess Louisa, then two years old. It was a disappointing, if not humiliating, honour. Gay rejected it, ceased to be a beggar of patronage three months before opening his opera that refers to men advancing themselves through bribes and flattery. Swift praised his friend for not dedicating the opera to a patron. Such 'wants I approve', wrote Swift on 26 February 1728. He also provided an explanation for the offer of a Gentleman Usher post to Gay in his 1729 'Vindication' of the playwright:

[Mr Gay] hath been somewhat singular in the Course of his Fortunes; for it hath happened, that after Fourteen Years attending the Court, with a large Stock of real Merit, a modest and agreeable Conversation, a Hundred Promises, and Five Hundred Friends, [Gay] hath failed of preferment, and upon a very weighty Reason. He lay under the Suspicion of having written a Libel or Lampoon against a great M[an or Minister, Walpole].

Advance word on *The Beggar's Opera* before its opening might have deterred offer of a higher court post. Seeking a producer for the new play, Gay first submitted the manuscript to Colley Cibber, manager of the prestigious Drury Lane theatre, friend of the court and later appointed poet laureate. Cibber could have told courtier friends about Gay's anti-government satire after he read it. Rejection by London's preeminent play producer was a blessing in disguise. Cibber's rival, John Rich, took the script and kept Gay free from court entanglement and possible requests from Cibber for line cuts. (As a theatre manager Cibber was notorious for demanding alterations from prospective authors.) No doubt Gay wrote against government corruption for more than personal reasons, but attribution of the play's authorship to a beggar was made by an author who had been a beggar.

The Satirist's Satirists

Walpole's regime outlived Gay (1685–1732), but Gay's most famous play outlived Walpole (1676–1745). Although it still is staged, *The Beggar's Opera* has aged. The first Minister is long gone, along with his corrupt patronage and financial chicanery. The topical satire of 1728, so popular and exciting in its day, was a novel sensation: a cheerful assault on local vice and the 'great' man known as Bob Booty. If the play still attracts interest on stage, that is due less to its satire of Walpole or opera than to character conflicts that transcend their time and place of origin. The rivalry between Peachum and Macheath after Polly marries the highwayman still can allure spectators; marriage, parenthood, romance, law remain obstacles and bothers to these men. The wit with which the two denigrate the morals and follies of their world might qualify them as satirists within a satire. In an environment where a beggar can become the author of an opera, why shouldn't an outlaw become a satirist, particularly if the audience shares his discontent with the law and its officials?

When Macheath tells Lucy that 'Money well tim'd, and properly apply'd, will do any thing', he wants money to bribe her father, the jailer. The line by itself is not so satiric. But then he starts singing to Lucy about how he can 'the Frown of a lady prevent' as the 'Perquisite softens her into Consent', and he is courting the young woman with witty lyrics. After hearing Air 33 Lucy agrees that 'What Love or Money can do shall be done'. Not only does his song win over the jailer's daughter, it also could corrupt a modern audience with pleasure, disarm them with the charm, humour and impudence of musical satire. If Macheath, playwright Gay and a small orchestra unite at such moments, it is not surprising that some of the author's contemporaries accused him of immoral and criminal activity. His critics thought him as dangerous as Macheath and Peachum because he wrote their winning speeches and songs. The historian Gibbon saw the comic side of this criticism when he argued that the popularity of *The Beggar's Opera* 'may, perhaps, have sometimes increased the number of highwaymen; but... it has had a beneficial effect in refining that class of men, making them... more like gentlemen' (Gay 1973: xix). While Macheath resembles a satirist as well as a gentleman at times, satirist Gay becomes a kind of highwayman as he deprives the wealthy and powerful of entitlement, gives it to thieves who would be like them. Mrs Peachum senses this situation and humorously objects to it when she asks 'what business' Captain Macheath has 'to keep Company with Lords and Gentlemen? He should leave them to prey upon one another' (2013: 9). (In fact, lords and gentlemen kept company with him by sitting onstage near the Captain, as seen in Blake's engraving.)

Looking at Gay's play from a modern perspective, we can see how this satire from the Long Eighteenth Century extended its reach to the present day even before Brecht adapted it for his stage. Mrs Peachum might be echoing a writer of her own age, Hobbes in *Leviathan*, when she describes the well-born as predators. But her husband unwittingly becomes a satirist of capitalism, far ahead of Marx, Brecht and Shaw, as he derides money's corrupting influence. Money is the only motive Mr Peachum can see behind Macheath's daring behaviour after he learns that the Captain has married Polly. (Love would never be considered a motive by him or Macheath.) 'Married! The Captain is a bold Man, and will risque anything for Money' (2013: 14). Here we have a little satire on the dangers of financial incentive. Peachum errs in his comic accusation, however; his new son-in-law does not crave wealth or a dowry but sex. (Would Freud on Thanatos, not Marx on capital, be the one to cite here?) Macheath risks his life by marrying Miss Peachum, as Empson has observed: 'the woman who really undoes him is not Jenny but Polly, however much against her will: unselfish love leads to honest marriage, and therefore Polly's father is determined to have him killed. It is love at its best that is the most fatal.' This 'may make it poetic justice that [Macheath] should betray her', as he does several times, in the sequel as well as the first instalment of the story (1975: 33).

But Macheath chooses to marry Polly. He weds women over and over again. In an acquisitive world expanding its trade and markets, Macheath acquires a total of five wives before the play ends. He seems to have lost count when he exclaims: 'What – four Wives more! This is too much – Here – tell the Sheriffs Officers I am ready' (2013: 68). Overwhelmed by the quantity of wives, Macheath turns his readiness to die into a satiric line, a comic rejection of his own excesses. He has other flashes of wit, too.

Polly's parents, despite their mordant response to other events, see little humour in their son-in-law's behaviour. While the new Mrs Macheath cannot live without her husband, her parents cannot live with him. She'll be as 'ill-us'd, and as much neglected, as if [she had] married a Lord!' protests her mother (a promising satirist herself) (2013: 14). Ever the business man, even as he contemplates having his son-in-law hanged Mr Peachum admires Macheath's criminal acumen. He calls the Captain 'a great Man', making him a Walpole of the underworld, and admits: 'it grieves one's Heart to take off a great Man. When I consider his Personal Bravery, his fine Stratagem, how much we have already got by him and how much more we may get, methinks I can't find in my Heart to have a Hand in his Death. I wish you could have made *Polly* undertake it' (2013: 21). This humorous anticipation of loss may be as close as Peachum comes to grief; he is no match for his daughter in the display of emotions.

The Peachums are too distressed to notice that they share with Macheath a talent for reciting exculpatory, witty maxims and song lyrics; but through them, John Gay's satire is appropriated by his characters. Though their morality may be objectionable, the clever lines spoken by these figures merge the language of London's underworld with that of its leading stage satirist. As if to confirm this association, Blake's depiction of the play in performance shows Gay standing near the scene on stage, almost unseen himself, but close enough to be a confederate. (See Figure 5 again, where the playwright stands against the wall to the left of a sculpted satyr.)

Witty as he may be, Jeremiah Peachum is also a man of business, for which reason he thinks no limits or laws should impede him. Crime is acceptable, even necessary at times; 'if Business cannot be carried on without it, what would you have a Gentleman do?' he asks his wife. (This viewpoint anticipates later satire in Brecht's *The Resistible Rise of Arturo Ui* and *Mother Courage*, the second of which its author said was 'meant to show' that war 'is a continuation of business by other means'; Brecht 1957: 220). Peachum's wits abet his crimes on occasion; his talent for surviving in a criminal world includes mastery of refined as well as coarse language. Speeches move from flattery to threats of blackmail, from quick repartees to rhymed song lyrics; they keep him in good standing with law officers, high society gentlemen and the criminal underworld. His business requires an understanding of wealthy clients, their taste and property. When Mr Peachum announces, 'I expect a Gentleman about this snuff box that Filch nimm'd two nights ago in the Park. I appointed him at this hour,' he is a punctual businessman prepared to return missing property to its owner for a price, a practice for which Jonathan Wild became famous and was hanged before Gay gave Peachum some Wild traits (2013: 40). The fence knows how to handle gentlemen's snuff boxes and handkerchiefs; he turns them into cash in a black-market operation that reverses the role gentlemen themselves play in support of the regular marketplace when they exchange pounds for luxuries.

Besides mocking forms of capital accumulation in London, *The Beggar's Opera* looks askance at romance as it was sentimentally represented in eighteenth-century stage plays. Mrs Peachum blames her daughter's infatuation on those 'curs'd Play-books she reads'. No particular play is named; but Gay offers an example of overwrought playwriting two scenes later (2013: 21), when Polly in a tearful monologue fears her new husband will go to the gallows, and indulges in visions of widowhood: 'Now I'm a Wretch, indeed. Methinks I see him already in the Cart, sweeter and more lovely than the Nosegay in his Hand!… The whole Circle are in Tears! – even the Butchers weep! – Jack Ketch [the hangman] himself hesitates to perform his Duty, and would be glad to lose his Fee, by a Reprieve. What then will become of Polly!' This rehearsal of grief, performed long before Macheath is scheduled to hang, could be performed as a parody of sentimental romance; but it is possible that Gay's audience and the actress portraying Polly took her speech seriously. Audiences loved the character's sentimentality, if the first ovation for Polly in 1728 is any indication of her appeal.

A Beautiful Beggar

Polly Peachum's character first won audience approval of Gay's play and her own dilemma when the actress Lavinia Fenton became a beautiful, plaintive beggar and sang Air 12. Pleading in song for her husband's life and her own, Polly (or the actress portraying her) also rescued the life of play, according to one account. Boswell, in his *Life of Johnson* (1923: 560), reports on this song's first reception, as he heard about it from actor James Quin:

> during the first night of its [the play's] appearance it was long in a very dubious state; that there was a disposition to damn it, and that it was saved by the song [Air 12]

> 'Oh ponder well! Be not severe!'

> the audience being much affected [Quin continues] by the innocent looks of Polly, when she came to those two lines, which exhibit at once a painful and ridiculous image,

> 'For on the rope that hangs my Dear
> Depends poor Polly's Life.'

As if responding to Polly's plea, the audience granted her and the play a reprieve with applause. She and Macheath would live onstage for many more nights. Gay's play subverts the seriousness of this scene and others through the contrast it offers between Polly's intensely earnest, heartfelt love for Macheath, and her husband's far from innocent life of crime, debauchery and maxims.

Captain Macheath later tells the audience that Polly 'is most confoundedly bit', meaning smitten by him; but the bite of love also brings with it some suffering, after Polly discovers she is competing with the jailer's daughter, Lucy, for the highwayman's devotion. 'Jealousy, Rage, Love and Fear are all at once tearing me to pieces,' laments Lucy. She tries to poison her rival in Act Three. 'I know she hates me!' confides Polly, as she declines to drink poison. Both women live to plead for Macheath's life during their prison visit, the scene Hogarth chose to paint (Act Three, Scene Eleven). In this scene and others where Polly and Lucy display heightened emotion, Gay was able to incorporate some of the sentiment, jealousy and abjection found in the period's 'curs'd Play-books' along with his own parody. As if he had intuited the appeal of Air 12, Polly's first plea for Macheath's life, Gay renews her entreaty and has her rival also plead in the prison scene. Air 54, another song from the distressed wife, is not quite a refrain of Air 12 but reminiscent of it: 'When my Hero in Court appears… think of poor Polly's Tears.' As part of the double-plea inside Newgate prison, Polly beseeches her father: 'Dear, dear Sir, sink the material Evidence, and bring him off at his Tryal – Polly upon her Knees begs it of you.' In response to this request, Polly's father says nothing. Lucy Lockit follows Polly's example, pleads with her father, the jailer, and claims, 'the Evidence is in your power'. She also sings. Both daughters plead; both fathers refuse. The double plea for withdrawal of incriminating evidence turns the women into singing beggars, but Peachum prefers to see them as prospective widows. With words fit for a satirist of sentiment, he responds to his daughter with outrageous consolation: 'Set your Heart at rest, Polly. Your Husband is to dye to-day. Therefore, if you are not already provided, 'tis high time to look for another. There's Comfort for you, you Slut' (2013: 64). The repeated display of sentimental love and pleading by Polly Peachum suggests that audience idolatry of her character was no accident; the playwright promoted her innocence while sending it up. Her father's cold, calculating responses constitute a variation of the satiric antipathy discussed earlier.

Ironically, Polly's pleas are later accepted by another beggar, the alleged author of the play, in Gay's closing scene. Faced with the prospect of Macheath's hanging, the Player declares:

Player: Why then, Friend, this is a down-right deep Tragedy. The Catastrophe is manifestly wrong, for an Opera must end happily.

Beggar: Your Objection, Sir, is very just; and is easily remov'd. For you must allow, that in this kind of Drama, 'tis no matter how absurdly things are brought about. So – you Rabble there – run and cry a Reprieve – let the Prisoner be brought back to his Wives in Triumph.

Player: All this we must do, to comply with the Taste of the Town. (2013: 69)

After efforts by three beggars, a 'down-right deep Tragedy' is averted and a happy ending with song and dance concludes the play. That Macheath in closing lines manages to endear himself to Polly and at the same time admire all his wives in the final song further affirms his gifts as a satirist.

Given his loving vow at the end of Part One to stay with Polly, 'And for Life, you slut', it is not surprising she pursues him across the world in Part Two (2013: 69). An indefatigably naïve and determined young woman in love, Polly confesses her undaunted passion in words that recall her father's; but she would not recite them with his cynicism: 'I did not marry [Macheath] (as 'tis the Fashion) coolly and deliberately for Honour or Money. But, I love him.' This naïve confession upsets Polly's mother so much that Mrs Peachum, in lines fit for the satirist she is, complains: 'I thought the Girl had been better bred' (2013: 15).

Serial Satire; or, the Return of Polly Peachum

While a number of John Gay's characters deliver derisive lines and reveal their own senses of humour as well as his, Polly Peachum is different. She seems incapable of speaking with cynicism. Again and again the sentiment voiced by Polly exposes her excessive naiveté, a willingness to believe both a romantic tale and a highwayman.

> **Polly:** Nay, my Dear, I have no Reason to doubt you, for I find in the Romance you lent me, none of the great Heroes were ever false in Love. (2013: 22)

In the sequel to *The Beggar's Opera*, Mrs Macheath (also known as Polly) overcomes great obstacles, and proves to be quite independent in pursuit of her husband as he evades the law and sundry women. Macheath claims he must leave her to avoid arrest. He assumes a new identity as the Black pirate Morano and evades her in the colonies in *Polly*. His wife doesn't recognize the black-faced man when she meets him abroad. The rest of the world around her (except for the indigenous tribe in Part Two) has little use for undivided love or loyalty. Others take interest in profitable ventures, highway robbery, gambling, sale of slaves.

While Mr Peachum proclaims that 'the greatest heroes have been ruin'd by women', Gay undermines such heroics (2013: 33). Being 'ruin'd by a woman', even a loving, loyal wife, does not necessarily make one a great hero, and Macheath in flight from Polly could be regarded as a comic anti-hero, a deserter and a rogue. His wife seems to have no idea that she endangers her husband by marrying him, or that he is near her and keeps his identity hidden in Part Two. So innocent is Polly that when she tries to lose her innocence abroad she fails. She disguises herself as a man to survive in the new world, and even in these circumstances, pretending to be manly, she secretly remains a young woman in love with a lawless, unfaithful husband. Gay's canny playwriting both exploits and subverts her sentimental love, and the extension of this practice in *Polly* confirms and amplifies its use in Part One. Had his sequel to *The Beggar's Opera* been permitted to open in 1729, *Polly* might have won audience adoration again as she did in 1728. Many of the sequel's songs concern love rather than politics. (An exception, Air 27, with its references to 'sneaking bribes', 'flattery and lies' of those who 'to power and grandeur rise' might have upset some courtiers had its performance been allowed.)

Over time *Polly* has received less attention and fewer productions than *The Beggar's Opera*. Its premiere was delayed decades due to censorship that kept it off the English stage from 1729 to 1777, and that hiatus certainly contributed to its neglect. Still it is important to note that by writing two plays for Polly and Macheath, John Gay, like Aristophanes in his writing, became a serial stage satirist. For Aristophanes, Cleon and Euripides were repeat offenders. In the prologue to *Polly*, the Poet argues that 'nobody can overdo it when he attacks the vice and not the person', a dictum that may explain Gay's return to political and social topics in the second of his 1728 stage plays. (He finished writing *Polly* before the end of that year.) He found his métier, and stayed with it, although the prologue to Part Two also mentions a fear that he will not be pardoned for imitating himself.

Gay was not the only one to proliferate representations of Polly. On 29 June 1728, the *Craftsman* reported on sales of 'The Beggar's Opera Screen: on which is curiously engrav'd on Copper-plates, the principal Captives of the All-conquering Polly'. The same day the journal featured a letter signed by Polly Peachum denying that she had published the pamphlets released under her name, except 'my Opera and Life, which were wrote by a Person that perform'd in the Beggar's Opera'. Miss Peachum's life was attracting ghostwriters, giving the playwright competition. Gay knew her fame was spreading by 20 March 1728, when he said in a letter to Jonathan Swift: 'There is a Mezzo-tinto Print publsh'd to day of Polly, the Heroine of the Beggar's Opera, who was before unknown & is now so high vogue, that I am in doubt whether her fame does not surpass that of the Opera itself.' If it seems too much attention has been given here to Miss Peachum, consider how much more she received in the first year of her life.

The prevention of *Polly*'s performance on stage in 1729 was probably what led John Gay to write another satire, *The Rehearsal at Goatham*, about a town that bans a puppet play before anyone has seen it. According to Gay's own 'advertisement', he based his plot on a 'Spanish treatise' by Gines de Passamonte commended by Cervantes. Gay says he 'has taken the liberty to make it comfortable with our own customs, and made England the scene of the farce'. To 'prevent particular persons from claiming general satire', he located the tale in 'a fictitious town, supposed to be remote from the great scenes of life' (1760: 365). With this disclaimer he could not be accused of writing a satire about London life or Walpole's fear of stage artists; but the play's discourse on the pre-emptive ban of a puppet show enables Gay to respond to and mock English theatre censorship. Peter the puppeteer's associate Pickle offers his audience brief excerpts from their banned play. His spectators protest that they are the ones depicted. 'Here's a rascal now,' says Sir Ninny in response to the puppeteer's introduction of a gambler who neglects his beautiful female companion. 'Hold, you dog,' adds Ninny, arguing the playwright within the play 'might as well have call'd me by my name... are family secrets to be divulg'd, rascal?' (1760: 387). His wife begs Ninny to say no more. While this rehearsal play is a minor work compared to Gay's first two ballad operas, it offers cogent, comic depiction of a process wherein satire finds its victims with their assistance. Regrettably the play written 1730–1 was unperformed in Gay's lifetime, and not published until 1754, twenty-two years after the author's death; like *Polly*, it has been neglected by producers.

Brecht Extends the Long Eighteenth Century

While John Gay wrote his own sequel to *The Beggar's Opera*, Bertolt Brecht's 1928 variant, *The Threepenny Opera*, became as least as famous as its source once it opened in Berlin. Brecht

(1898–1956) reutilized Gay's characters and some of their original story after his assistant and collaborator, Elisabeth Hauptmann, provided a translation. Her attention was brought to the ballad opera by Nigel Playfair's 1920 Lyric Theatre, Hammersmith revival which ran for three years. Playfair cut and adapted Gay's text, but not as radically as Brecht, who in turn inspired other, later rewritings by Vaclav Havel (Czechoslovakia), Wole Soyinka (Nigeria), Dario Fo (Italy), Ajitesh Bandyopadhyay (India) and Carl Grose (England). The aggregate history of these texts suggests that stage satire need not go out of date if topical issues and musical fashions change; there are ways to revitalize and reuse a 'classic' so that it continues to speak to new audiences. Brecht led the way, turning Gay's eighteenth-century satire into three new works. He gave the work so many new lives that, rephrasing Marx's paraphrase of Hegel, which argued 'all facts and personages of great importance in world history occur, as it were, twice... the first time as tragedy, the second as farce' (1963: 5), we might note that the facts and personages of Gay's stage satire returned the first time as *The Threepenny Opera*; the second time as Brecht's screenplay for *The Threepenny Opera*; the third time as Brecht's *Threepenny Novel*. The German term for this reutilization is *Umfunktionierung*, and Brecht was a master of it (Mayer 1971: 89) (Figure 6).

For him and other modern theatre artists, notably directors Vsevolod Meyerhold and Joan Littlewood, satire was a continuing practice; it could begin with someone else's play, and with adaptation its timeliness need not end after one season in the theatre or even one century. Meyerhold innovatively revived Gogol's satire *The Government Inspector*, adding new speeches and a new look to it, and Brendan Behan engaged in this creative process with Littlewood, revising and expanding his own play, *The Hostage*, as will be seen later.

Gay's continuation of *The Beggar's Opera* in *Polly* also returns in an intriguing modern sequel by Wole Soyinka. The Nigerian playwright's *Opera Wonyosi* (1977) finds African equivalents to the criminal underworld of Gay's first ballad opera and to scenes of slave trade and colonial occupation in

Polly. Also indebted to Brecht's version of *The Beggar's Opera*, Soyinka turns not only to literature, but also to African history. As a writer who endured British colonial rule, then witnessed misrule in postcolonial Africa, he portrays new corruption. His Macheath calls incompetent subordinates 'cannibals', and rumours of cannibalism practiced by the dictator of a new African nation give this insult resonance. Asked whether his gang stole wedding goods, the new Macheath replies, 'All this stuff has been merely liberated' (1981: 15). A key word of the African independence movement, 'liberation' becomes a euphemism for theft in a postcolonial society. Liberation movements created to free Africa from oppressors and Western dominance give way to new abuse of power and language that excuses it. To abet his satire of national leaders and misdeeds in the 1970s, Soyinka locates events in the Central African Republic where Bokassa is being crowned. The play refers to Ugandan and Nigerian scandals, too. A Nigerian civil war exile named Dee-Jay and Emperor Bokassa offer comic patter that Soyinka's first audience at the University of Ife might have appreciated more than outsiders seeing it now.

Brecht's stage adaptation of Gay was different. The German playwright set his characters in Victorian London, not Gay's eighteenth-century city or his own Berlin. The resulting dislocation made the play less pointed in topical satire than Soyinka's or Gay's; but its scenes have remained accessible to those who (like Brecht's original spectators) do not live in Victorian London. He makes no direct reference to living individuals except the Queen of England, and that lack of specificity could have contributed to *The Threepenny Opera*'s international popularity. Brecht's practices of Epic Theatre, although not fully developed in 1928, turn his distancing of place and time to advantage. Answering a question Giorgio Strehler asked him about the play's location, Brecht said: 'A good deal was known about the Victorian age, which at the same time was remote enough to be judged with critical detachment, thus permitting the audience to pick out what was relevant to them' (1979: 100–1). Brecht wanted

Figure 6 *Bertolt Brecht in his Berlin flat, 1927.*

spectators to share his 'delight in comparison, in distance, in dissimilarity', and so they did in Berlin by welcoming his satire set in London of 1838, the date of Queen Victoria's coronation (1957: 276).

Raymond Williams thought that *The Threepenny Opera*'s 'portraits of a society trying to pass itself off as respectable' did not shock or 'penetrate the established false consciousness' of its Berlin audience. 'Nothing is more predictable... than the conscious enjoyment of a controlled and distanced low life.' The whores and thieves in Brecht's play were seen by 'respectable playgoers' as 'licensed types' in 'a special class, a district', while the audience's 'ordinary view of life' remained safe. 'The play in fact fitted easily into "what the spectator wishes to see": crime and coldness not structural in the society, but lived out in a romantic and theatrical district' (Williams 1979: 192–3).

In response to Williams, it could be argued that spectatorship itself and the audience's 'ordinary view of life' are mocked by Brecht's satire. The play wryly depicts the business interests of its central characters, too, but Jeremiah Peachum's business is linked to spectatorship and theatre art early in the play. Peachum trains and costumes his employees for roles as beggars; they unwittingly become actors in what Brecht elsewhere defined as Aristotelean theatre. The beggars solicit money but for that they have to win empathy from their audience. Mr Peachum has reservations about this practice. 'My business is too hard, for my business is arousing human sympathy' (1979: 4). Employees of the 'Beggar's Friend Ltd' help him produce the 'five basic types of misery, those likely to touch the human heart', and they profit from misery if they win financial assistance from passers-by (1979: 8). The problem with selling misery as a commodity, Peachum admits and Brecht underscores with humour, is that the world sees too much suffering. The novelty and shock of it wear out, much like the bite of topical satire. 'You just haven't any idea! Obviously I can't extend your engagement,' Peachum tells one of his beggars, as if he is firing an actor (1979: 30). Something new was needed by Brecht, too; but his business turned out to be quite different from Peachum's. Through Epic and dialectical theatre he sought to reduce empathy, increase independent thought and consciousness of the need for social change – for performers and spectators, satire was one means towards that end.

Brecht directs his satire in *The Threepenny Opera* at the world of businessmen as well as spectatorship; at times the two targets merge. Macheath and Polly take on new roles, and see the world differently after he decides to become a banker and she becomes a businesswoman.

Polly Peachum, Capitalist

Polly Peachum learns to handle money in *The Threepenny Opera*. First she is forced to give up a brief career as an actress. After she sings 'Pirate Jenny' at her wedding, Macheath warns his wife: 'I didn't like your playacting; let's not have any more of it' (1979: 22). Her ability to transform herself, the playacting of which Macheath disapproves, is shown in the song where she becomes a fierce pirate ship commander and previews her ability to take charge of a modern crew, Macheath's gang. Later when a gang member doubts that a woman can direct Mack the Knife's men, Polly summons the kind of anger already shown by Pirate Jenny. 'Of course you're not saying anything against me!' she screams (1979: 38). The rest of the gang applauds her performance.

Before Polly's innocence and naiveté fully disappear, she shows some trepidation about her husband's fidelity and safety; but after a few scenes the new Mrs Macheath becomes her father's daughter – a no-nonsense, take-no-prisoners business person. She literally takes no prisoners when she visits Macheath in jail in Act Three, and says she can't afford to rescue him from hanging. The money that might go to bribes was transferred to Manchester after her husband advised Polly to send 'the profits to Jack Poole's banking house in Manchester' (1979: 37). Cash-poor Polly mentions that she might be able to put a word in with the Queen on Mack's behalf. It seems like a polite lie, given the tentative, quick delivery of the line; but a reprieve from Queen Victoria arrives and saves Macheath's life on coronation day. We never learn whether Polly's newly acquired leadership position entitled her to favours from her Highness. But even if she cannot command a royal audience, she takes command of her husband's financial holdings with aplomb. The satire here quietly subverts patriarchy, as Mrs Macheath and the Queen of England rule and Mack the Knife needs their help in the closing scenes. A complaint made about Polly by her father early in the play turns out to be a comic prophecy: 'So now she's associating with criminals. That's lovely. That's delightful' (1979: 28).

It is surprising the playwright does not allow the actress in Polly's role to step out of character when asked by Mack about money to bribe his jailers. She could first repeat 'the business is doing very well... the money has gone off to Manchester... I have got nothing on me' (1979: 72–3), and then she could turn to the audience and say, as Brecht once did: 'Comrades, let us talk about the conditions of property ownership' (Brecht 2003: 162). Macheath does this instead, as we will see.

Max Spalter noted that 'Brecht wished, among other things, to make *The Threepenny Opera* a piece of forceful anticapitalistic satire'. His anti-capitalist attitude contributes to the play's 'predominately negative tone that can be described as racy and cynical, raffish and knowing, bawdy and mocking' (1967: 176). A few years before writing *Threepenny* Brecht had decided Karl Marx 'was the only spectator for my plays I'd ever come across… A man with interests like his must of necessity be interested in my plays' (1957: 24). Walter Benjamin suggested that Marx's writings on capitalism inspired satire, and 'it is with Marx that Brecht has gone to school' (1977: 84). Brecht wanted his plays to foster critical thought instead of sympathy; and alternatives to capitalism, instead of ruthless financial profit. He said this in essays, but his preferences also can be read between the lines of *The Threepenny Opera*, particularly in the scenes that call attention to Polly and Macheath's banking.

Brecht's Banker, Macheath

Had Marx been in the audience the night *The Threepenny Opera* opened, he might have been amused by Macheath's decision to become a banker. 'It's safer and it's more profitable' than his other businesses, he tells Polly in one of their more intimate discussions (1979: 37). By bringing a legendary criminal into the world of banking and corporate capitalism (more fully in his *Threepenny* screenplay and novel than in the 1928 stage play), Brecht gave Mack the Knife a modern perspective on crime. Satiric playwriting amplified the author of *Capital*'s economic and social criticism, especially through Macheath's gallows speech, another significant departure from Gay's play. Lamenting the inability of a small-time racketeer to compete with large corporate entities, the gangster steps out of character on stage at the time he is scheduled to hang and says:

> We lower middle-class artisans … are being swallowed up by big corporations backed by banks. What's breaking into a bank compared with founding a bank? What's murdering a man compared with hiring a man? (1979: 76)

Disrupting the suspense of the play here, the actor portraying Macheath steps out of his prison cage to address the audience about social and financial conditions that have brought the condemned man to this turn. It is a wry self-conscious moment, where the playwright threatens his character with obsolescence rather than death, or with death by obsolescence – an inability to sustain his criminal career in a society that gives large syndicates license to profitably buy, sell and dispose of human life.

Like this satiric speech relegating Mackie's gang of 'lower middle-class artisans' to the annals of history, the play as a whole shows an old-fashioned outlaw losing stature and his ability to outmanoeuvre rival profiteers who have the law on their side. When the Knife interrupts the plot to say this with self-conscious theatricality, Brecht's satire of capitalism and theatre coincide; theatre itself, spectatorship and the climactic build towards a hanging are disrupted and mocked. This self-conscious and self-critical intervention precedes another mockery of the play's structure, the royal pardon, and then another abrupt shift follows Macheath's rescue. Instead of Gay's blithe ending, where the reprieved highwayman dances and sings about retiring with one woman, in *The Threepenny Opera* a happy ending is averted. Although Polly says she is content, her father warns that rescues like Macheath's occur all too rarely, especially for the poor whose fates 'only can be grim'. The chorus then concludes with a hymn about injustice, death and winter storms, a song so dark it constitutes black humour to sing it just after a man's life has been saved. The grim finale ends: 'Think of the blizzards and the black confusion / Which in this vale of tears we must behold' (1979: 79). (The ensemble finale also sends up the high art of a Bach chorale.)

Macheath's rescue is hardly celebrated, but then neither is the man himself, at least not by Brecht. In notes on the play, the author described Macheath as a staid businessman, portly rather than handsome. Photographs of the 1928 production support his view of the character; actor Harald Paulson's Macheath looks like a solemn, drably clothed Berliner in modern coat and trousers. Berating gang members that they'll never be businessmen and they have no table manners, aloof and moody, the 1928 Macheath is not particularly admirable. His brusque demeanour corresponds to an attitude Brecht found in Swift's pamphlet *A Modest Proposal* (1729). Writing about the difficulties of truth telling in 1934, the German author sees nastiness employed as a means of satire in Swift's proposal to sell infants as edible delicacies; the Irish satirist 'defended a particular mode of thinking, which he detested, with great fire and thoroughness, and in a discussion of an issue where all its nastiness would be fully recognizable to anyone' (2003: 152). Comparable churlishness and the profit motive it satirizes can be seen in Macheath the prospective banker, whose 'particular mode of thinking' Brecht probably detested.

Accounts of opening night in Berlin indicate the audience first became vehement in its enthusiasm for *The Threepenny Opera* during performance of 'The Cannon Song', in which Macheath and his British army companion (now Sheriff of London) Tiger Brown sing about their military adventures in India. Here too the satire is nasty, as the army veterans recall how they destroyed local populations, people of colour. Their musical paean to racist, imperial violence accompanied by Kurt Weill's infectious, strident music makes it sound as if the men had a rollicking good time before companions died; with irony, male bonding over murder becomes the cause for song and dance at a wedding. The men preface their raucous hymn to colonial occupation with words of nostalgia, and sing under a 'golden glow' of light, softness that makes the brash song even more jarring (1979: 23). John Gay's ballad opera first won audiences over with Polly Peachum's musical plea to save her husband's life. In Berlin, where inflation and unemployment existed alongside exceptional wealth and avant-garde culture, the winning song was appropriately harsh in its imagery, and joyous in its music. Its last stanza about soldiers dying hardly endorsed army life. After the song, Macheath admits it is not an old friendship that protects him from the law, but payoffs to the sheriff in return for advance warning about police raids. So much for sentiment.

In 'The Cannon Song' and others, Kurt Weill's music with parodic refrains of tango, jazz and military marches contributed to *The Threepenny Opera*'s popularity. Brecht's lyrics and the new music gave songs a modern, acid humour; they were hardly Victorian, particularly not 'Mack the Knife'. Inspired by a German street ballad, its stanzas about a criminal who keeps his hands clean much as a shark keeps its teeth white have not lost any irony over time, as white-collar criminals (including bankers Macheath would admire) perfect the art of unindictable financial killings. John Willett observed that Kurt Weill's orchestration in *The Threepenny Opera* 'becomes a kind of punctuation, an underlining of the words, a well-aimed comment giving the gist of the action or the text. And that remains its prime function in all Brecht's plays' (1968: 132). But the 'kind-of-speaking-against-the-music' Brecht sought from singers allowed his lyrics to be separated somewhat from the music so songs can sound dissonant, if not downright nasty (Brecht 1964: 45).

His play differs considerably from John Gay's, but Brecht once claimed that 'Under the title *The Beggar's Opera, The Threepenny Opera* has been performed for the past two hundred years in theatres throughout England' (1977: 321–2). Through either comic arrogance, subtle joking or to simplify a complicated process of adaptation, Brecht suggests he and John Gay wrote the same play. He admits it has a new score, but claims both authors faced 'the same sociological situation', and people are still 'living off morality, not leading a moral

life'. Brecht sees a continuity from Gay's satire to his. Certainly
there are significant differences between the texts, but the
practice of appropriating another satirist's work appealed
to Brecht. For the satire in *Puntila and His Servant Matti* he
found inspiration in Chaplin's *City Lights* and a play by Hella
Wuolijoki. He appropriated the title character of Jaroslav
Hasek's satiric novel for his play set in a later period – *Schweyk
in the Second World War*. He also reutilized Farquhar's *The
Recruiting Officer* for *Trumpets and Drums*, adapted Moliere's
Don Juan, and drew on Shakespeare for some satire in *The
Resistible Rise of Arturo Ui*.

The Theatricality of Fascism

In a number of these plays, Brecht returns to themes of *The
Threepenny Opera*. After writing a play, novel and screenplay
about Macheath, he moves on to satirize other businessmen and -women who aspire to respectability and profit at
great cost to others. In *Puntila and His Servant Matti,* the
wealthy estate owner Puntila becomes intoxicated and repents
exploiting employees, including his chauffeur, Matti. When
he sobers up, the master retracts his generous words, exhibits
contradictions and division within himself also shown less
satirically by Shen Teh, the tobacco shop owner in *The Good
Person of Szechwan*. Puntila's role requires physical dexterity
akin to Chaplin's, as he goes from drunkenness to sobriety
and back again, a cycle also shown in *City Lights*. Matti's role
requires mental dexterity, deadpan adjustments to Puntila's
whims: 'When I'm talking with my employers, I never have any
opinions, they don't like the help to have opinions,' he admits.
Like the good soldier Schweyk, he follows orders even when
they go against his employer's interests (1976: 110). Written in
1940, *Puntila* was not performed until 1948. The play suffered
a delayed opening due to the author's exile and the disruptions
of world war.

A more topical satire, *Schweyk in the Second World War*, which shows Hitler seeking assistance from the 'Little Man' Schweyk near Stalingrad, was written 1941–3 but not staged until 1957. *The Resistible Rise of Arturo Ui*, a parable about the rise of Hitler written to ridicule the German leader in 1941, was not staged until 1958. As Brecht observed in his essay 'Five Difficulties in Writing the Truth', truth 'cannot simply be written; you absolutely have to write it for someone, someone who is able to use it' (2003: 148). Deprived of theatre audiences that spoke German during his years of exile, Brecht finally was able to use these plays after he and his wife, actress Helene Weigel, founded their own theatre, the Berliner Ensemble, in 1949.

Even if his parable about Hitler had been staged in the early 1940s, *The Resistible Rise of Arturo Ui* would not have responded adequately to threats posed by the German leader and his army. Arturo Ui's plan to take over Chicago's vegetable market with the violence of Al Capone is small-time crime compared to Hitler's assault on Europe. Chaplin also tried to satirize the Nazi dictator's ambitions in his film *The Great Dictator*, released in 1939. In retrospect, both Brecht's effort and Chaplin's fared best when they focused on the man himself, his preposterous, operatic public speaking. The horrors of Nazi warfare and mass murder do not lend themselves to humour. But *Arturo Ui*, if viewed as a response to the language and gestures of tyranny, still offers some instructive satire about 'the theatricality of fascism'. Ui's acting lesson in scene six and his subsequent tirades in the play illustrate this term which was first defined in Brecht's *Messingkauf* dialogues. In one of these dialogues (not written for *Arturo Ui*) two characters discuss how Hitler's fiery speeches and fascist theatricality induce 'everyone to abandon their own points of view'. Listeners 'adopt [the speaker's viewpoint]... forget their own interests... He involves his audience in himself, implicates them in his movements, lets them "participate" in his troubles and triumphs, and dissuades them from any criticism, even from a fleeting glance at their surroundings from their own viewpoint'

(2003: 198–9). Brecht's Epic Theatre and his satiric theatre
achieve the opposite effect, as they distance the audience from
empathy, encourage antipathy and laughter. Through satiric
impersonation an actor can take control of a tyrant like Ui,
bend and shape the character in situations that reduce his or
her power.

Arturo Ui takes on some of Hitler's physical traits and shows
the 'theatricality of fascism' in a grotesque, comic scene where
he studies acting to improve his public image. He wants people
to look at him and forget everyone else when he is speaking. A
dictator thrives on public attention; complete attention could
bring total control. Before Brecht wrote the scene, he may have
watched Chaplin's *The Great Dictator*. Ui's acting teacher
advises, 'You don't want to look like a barber', as if to warn
against one of the two roles Chaplin played in his film. (The other
role, Adenoid Hynkel, was Hitler with a Chaplin moustache.)
Coached by an old-fashioned, second-rate actor in Scene Six,
Arturo Ui becomes a clownish copy of Hitler. 'Perhaps if you
joined your arms in front of your private parts... Not bad.
Relaxed but firm,' counsels his instructor (1976: 141). Ui may
look foolish and sound like a poorly trained Shakespearean
actor, but that does not prevent the clown from speaking with
the fury of a tyrant, as Jan Kott noted of a Warsaw *Arturo Ui*
production where the actor Lomnicki

> gets angry, rages. His movements are still mechanical,
> limited, clownish. But he has an entourage. Men in long
> coats, revolvers in their pockets... the clown is for hire, and
> so are the murderers... He has not ceased to be a clown, but
> he has also become Hitler. It is one of the greatest scenes I
> have seen in the theatre – and one of the most terrifying...
> From the first to the last scene he is a clown; but not once
> does he make the audience laugh. (Kott 1968: 109)

Brecht anticipated this production (which he never saw) in
notes about *The Resistible Rise of Arturo Ui*. He rejected the
idea 'that satire should not meddle in serious matters... Serious

things are precisely its concern. The great political criminals must be thoroughly stripped bare and exposed to ridicule. Because they are not great political criminals at all, but the perpetrators of great political crimes, which is something different' (1976: 456). *Arturo Ui* went unstaged, unable to expose political criminals to ridicule in the 1940s, but in 1959 the play received an acclaimed production at the Berliner Ensemble, with Brecht's son-in-law Ekkehard Schall in the role of Ui. Lomnicki's Warsaw performance followed in 1963.

Idols and False Messiahs

Long after Hitler's defeat and Brecht's efforts to ridicule him, the dictator (or his impersonator) arrived on a Broadway stage in 2001 and stayed there for six years in Mel Brooks's comedy, *The Producers*. If the goal was to have audiences laugh at Hitler, the play was sixty years late. But much of Brooks's humour came from his mockery of commercial theatre producers who invest in a play full of *kitsch* titled *Springtime for Hitler*. Driven by a profit motive, the producers want to offend their audience so the show will close overnight and they can hold on to unspent investor funds. The show fails to fail, the audience finds its campy outrages humorous and the producers end up in jail for fraud. Producing a play on Broadway becomes a criminal act.

Broadway producers also engaged in fraud in an earlier American satire, *Messiah in America* (1933), by Yiddish American satirist Moishe Nadir. The play deserves some recognition in the annals of satire for its prescient view of a consumer culture where almost anything can be bought and sold. Nadir's show businessmen, desperate to sell tickets, announce a Messiah's arrival at their New York theatre. A second false messiah appears in a Coney Island amusement park. The two saviours face off in a boxing ring, and the winner is declared the true messiah, anticipating an era (our own) in which truth is relative and show business is able to confer fame and fortune. Brooks's Hitler impersonator views the world almost the same way when he sings: 'It ain't no mystery / If it's politics or history. / The thing you gotta know is, / Everything is show biz' (Brooks 2001: 187). By the start of the twenty-first century (and earlier in Nadir's 1933 satire) America was a place where show business could turn men and women into idols. A popular talent competition televised weekly was called *American Idol*. By 2020, the White House itself had become a centre for show business and self-idolatry, with the President boasting about his television ratings. By repeatedly broadcasting electronic messages (Tweets), Trump gave new form to the theatricality of fascism described by Brecht. In self-praise and prejudices shared with millions through Tweets, he 'involves his audience in himself, implicates them in his movements, lets them "participate" in his troubles and triumphs, and dissuades them from any criticism, even from a fleeting glance at their surroundings from their own viewpoint' (Brecht 2003: 198–9).

One other satiric response to fascism by Brecht in the 1940s remains all too timely. Not conceived as a stage play, *Conversations in Exile* was adapted by Howard Brenton for a London theatre production by Foco Novo in 1983, and recently published under the title of *Refugee Conversations* in a new English translation by Romy Fursland. The dialogues about forced exile and flight from war have regrettably taken on new resonance as large groups of people around the world seek refuge from climate change crises, civil wars, poverty and hunger. Sardonic exchanges Brecht wrote for two exiles named Kalle and Ziffel refer to Nazi tyranny, but some of their conversations anticipate current emergencies and the extraordinary demands made on those who want to survive hardship in our time. Ziffel expresses a longing for ordinary life and a world that doesn't require heroism:

> what are we poor human beings to do... All across the continent heroic deeds are on the increase, the achievements

of the common man are ever more tremendous, a new virtue is invented every day. To obtain a single sack of flour nowadays you need the same amount of energy with which you'd once have been able to farm a whole province... Homeric courage is required to walk down the street; the self-denial of Buddha is needed if you even want to be tolerated... Only by showing the humanity of a Francis of Assisi can you keep yourself from murdering someone. The world has become an abode for heroes, so where are we to go? (2020: 93)

In Brecht's *Galileo*, the title character warns: 'Unhappy is the land that needs a hero' (1961: 392). Those words and the refugee dialogues suggest another tenet for an aesthetics of satire. Where Aristotelian tragedy calls for a hero, or at least a protagonist who suffers, satire does not. Gay's Macheath and Brecht's Mack the Knife, and the refugees Ziffle and Kalle in *Conversations*, are not heroes but survivors. Fleeing those who would hold them captive in London and Hitler's Europe, they become outsiders, flight risks.

Inquisitive, looking into the origins of world war, wealth inequality and revolution gone astray, Brecht and fellow satirists Nicolai Erdman, Vladimir Mayakovsky and Karl Kraus responded to extremes and deprivations that made it difficult to celebrate heroism, or even maintain the 'decency' and 'logic' Brecht once associated with Shaw's humour (Brecht 1957: 10). Twentieth-century upheavals led Brecht and company to portray men and women less comfortable with their way of life than the arms manufacturer Undershaft in Shaw's *Major Barbara* (1905) or the thieves in John Gay's ballad opera. Gay's Peachum, for example, declares murder 'as fashionable a Crime as a man may be guilty of' and fit for 'many fine Gentlemen'. His frivolity might not be so welcome in response to the slaughter and government lies characteristic of the world war Karl Kraus portrayed in his play *The Last Days of Mankind,* a precursor of *Refugee Conversations* and other writings by Brecht.

Karl Kraus's Last Days

Witnessing battlefield casualties and amputations performed without anaesthesia when he served as a medical orderly in 1918, Brecht saw the horrors of the First World War first-hand. He saw how satire could respond to these horrors and to the high-placed advocates of war when he read Karl Kraus's gargantuan play, *The Last Days of Mankind* (1922). In fifty-five scenes plus prologue and epilogue reconstructing the lethal follies of the First World War, including self-serving statements by journalists, generals and profiteers, Kraus provided Brecht with inspiration for the caustic battlefield conversations in *Mother Courage, A Man's a Man, Schweyk in the Second World War* as well as *Refugee Conversations*. A 1943 entry in Brecht's daily journal records that he 'would like to do *Schweyk* interspersed with scenes from *The Last Days of Mankind* so people can see the ruling forces up top with the private soldier down below surviving all their vast plans' (1994: xiii). Clearly he had not forgotten Kraus's play while exiled in Santa Monica, California. Years earlier the Viennese satirist Kraus visited rehearsals of *The Threepenny Opera* in Berlin and suggested some song lyrics before the play opened in 1928.

'Brecht, like Kraus, teaches by grotesque example,' Max Spalter observes in *Brecht's Tradition* (1967: 183). Both playwrights refer ironically to the 'great' war 'victories' won through great suffering, and the unequal distribution of wealth and privilege that accompanies such victories. Their plays give voices to the victims of war and its objectors not often quoted in history books. Kraus's satire differs from Brecht's in its heavy reliance on actual First World War events and quotations as source material. He acknowledges in a preface to *The Last Days of Mankind*: 'The most improbable actions reported here really occurred... The most improbable conversations conducted here were spoken word for word' (2015: 1). Kraus was truly a satirist of his times, as he drew on press reports, casualty statistics, declarations of victory and other government propaganda for the outrageous dialogue and action in his play. He also exercised his imagination, writing lines to be spoken by gas masks, a dying forest and soldiers frozen to death; but many of his characters turn verbatim statements of men at war into satire, a facility lucidly summarized by Walter Benjamin when he wrote: 'Kraus creeps into those he impersonates, in order to annihilate them' (1999: 442).

Soviet Satire: Bulgakov, Erdman, Mayakovsky, Meyerhold

Benjamin also commended Kraus's 'struggle against the empty phrase', a struggle shared by a few satirists in the Soviet Union who initially welcomed the Russian Revolution, had their new plays subsidized by the state and then saw the state turn against them when they humorously criticized it in the 1920s and 1930s (1999: 434). Vsevolod Meyerhold, Vladimir Mayakovsky, Nicolai Erdman and Mikhail Bulgakov did not fare well under Stalin after their comic depiction of misguided comrades. They saw more humour than the state did in its bureaucratic language and plans inspired by Marx, Lenin and the 'New Economic Policy'. Bulgakov (discussed briefly in Chapter 1) responded to the state's new economic experiment in private enterprise by setting *Madame Zoya* (1927) in a brothel (a private enterprise) disguised as a dressmaker's shop. Plays by Mayakovsky and Erdman ridiculed bureaucracy, fetishism of party lines and official language designed, as George Orwell later complained, 'to make lies sound truthful and murder respectable, and to give an appearance of solidity to pure wind' (Orwell 1953: 171). Erdman mocked citizens who dreamed of restoring monarchy to Russia and a man who pretends to be a Communist Party member in *The Mandate* (1925). Meyerhold directed the premiere of that satire as well as Mayakovsky's *The Bedbug* (1929), which showed petty bourgeois characters pursuing a marriage of convenience to acquire working-class affiliation. 'Don't call me Comrade, Madame Citizen!' Prisypkin warns his future mother-in law, 'your daughter hasn't married into the proletariat yet!' (Mayakovsky 1968: 146). In *The Bath House* (1930), another Mayakovsky satire directed by Meyerhold, a Soviet bureaucrat refuses to fund a time machine and finds himself left behind after time-travellers blast off into the future (Figure 7). The bureaucrat, Pobedonosikov, wonders aloud if this means he will have no role in the future of Communism. For implying an affirmative answer, Mayakovsky and Meyerhold were severely reproached by the state-sponsored press. 'At that time some influential critics were suggesting that satire did nothing but harm the cause of socialism,' according to Edward Braun (1969: 258). Following negative reviews of *The Bath House*, Mayakovsky committed suicide in April of 1930, in part because of a disappointing love affair, but also due to his loss of standing as a pro-Soviet writer. Meyerhold was subsequently denied artistic support by the state. In 1939–40 he was arrested, accused of treason and executed.

Figure 7 *Meyerhold and Mayakovsky's* The Bath House, *Moscow, 1930.*

Meyerhold's troubles with the Kremlin and the adverse criticisms of his stage direction were not limited to his production of new plays. In 1926 he staged a revival of Gogol's classic Russian satire, *The Government Inspector*. The director altered the text and added some speeches from other sources; but his most innovative improvements were visual. Set designs allowed tableaux of actors to move downstage on platforms while the cast stood still, creating the stage equivalent of cinematic close-ups. Grotesque comic acting and meticulously detailed crowd scenes amplified the inept and crooked behaviour of Gogol's town folk. Meyerhold's portrayal of corruption among Russian officials in a provincial nineteenth-century town made no explicit suggestion that comparable or greater abuses in governance were taking place under Stalin's rule. Denying that this *Inspector* presentation was 'a metaphor for the rise of Stalin', David Chambers notes that the director left behind only one sentence hinting he addressed contemporary conditions through Gogol's play: 'With this production, we shall cleanse the Soviet system' (Chambers 1998: 55). Later Meyerhold was accused of 'formalism' for his departures from socialist realism, also of favouring Trotsky over Stalin. 'Satire', 'Gogol' and *The Bath House* were not officially listed among Meyerhold's crimes, but his irreverence towards bureaucracy and his nonconformity as a 'formalist' director turned Stalinists against him.

Soviet interference with satire was no laughing matter, with one exception: a cabaret sketch titled *A Meeting about Laughter*, co-authored by Nicolai Erdman and Nicholas Mass, and published not long before Erdman was sent to a Siberian labour camp in 1933. At the start of the sketch, a speaker announces to his comrades that 'we need joyous, cheerful art, and that we must do something to make spectators in the theatre laugh'. Politically acceptable attitudes towards laughter are proposed by one Communist delegate after another. They debate with solemnity, and do not appear susceptible to laughter themselves. One speaker warns his audience: 'I see that a few of those present are grinning. Shame on you, comrades! There is nothing to grin about when I am speaking to you about such an important sector of laughter' (1995: 167). Erdman found humour in prohibitions, even in death. In his play titled *The Suicide*, different characters claim that a suicide note was written to support their cause. This satire attracted interest from Stanislavsky and Meyerhold, but it could not be staged in the Soviet Union during Erdman's lifetime. (He lived until 1970.) One character sums up the repression of Soviet art in the 1930s when he explains the reason so many others care about the contents of the suicide note: 'Nowadays only the dead may say what the living think' (Erdman 1979: 18). Still alive after changing his mind and deciding he has no reason to commit suicide, Semyon Semyonovich Podseknalnikov makes a heterodox, anti-heroic announcement: 'I do not want to die, comrades. Not for you, not for them, not for the class struggle, not for humanity' (1979: 51). This defiant confession was not heard onstage in Russia until 1990, when Yuri Lyubimov staged Erdman's play at Moscow's Taganka Theatre during the advent of *perestroika* – a time of 'reconstruction' and increased artistic freedom. For a few years in the 1980s all of Lyubimov's productions were banned in Russia and Lyubimov himself was deprived of citizenship between 1984 and 1989, which may constitute a backhanded affirmation of his independence as a theatre artist, more overtly affirmed by his staging of *The Suicide*.

Smaller Stages: Karl Valentin, Liesl Karlstadt, Erika Mann, *Beyond the Fringe*

Erdman's sketch on laughter was one of many cabaret satires written in the 1920s and 1930s, a period of increasing authoritarianism in the Soviet Union and Europe. While the primary focus of this study is three full-length plays and their background, it would be an oversight not to mention a few satiric sketches and cabaret acts that influenced full-length stage satires in the twentieth century. Brecht acknowledged the importance to him of cabaret clowning by Karl Valentin and his cross-dressing partner Liesl Karlstadt in Munich. Their acts mocked misguided firemen, musicians and photographers, and Brecht collaborated with them more than once on small projects.

Brecht also knew performers in the Peppermill, a satiric troupe directed by Erika Mann that began in Munich and had to go into exile after the Nazis took power. He later worked with two of the group's artists: actress Therese Giehse and eccentric dancer Lotte Goslar. Mann's satire of Nazis took allegorical and musical forms. One song about Hitler's foreign policies was titled 'The Prince of Liarland' (Senelick 1993: 251). Peppermill's cabaret satire was reimagined in the play *Mephisto*, based in part on a novel by Erika Mann's brother Klaus, and performed by Ariane Mnouchkine's theatre troupe, Theatre du Soleil, in France in 1979.

Brendan Behan and Joan Littlewood, discussed in the next chapter, drew inspiration from pantomime and music hall acts when creating plays at Theatre Workshop in the late 1950s and early 1960s. The English theatre world that welcomed Behan and Littlewood's satire also applauded *Beyond the Fringe* (1960–6), an evening of sketches assembled by four gifted comedians: Jonathan Miller, Peter Cook, Dudley Moore and Alan Bennett. The quartet debunked politicians, concert pianists, Shakespearean actors and themselves. Their arrival was preceded and influenced by *The Goon Show* (1951–60), madcap radio adventures featuring Peter Sellers, Harry Secombe, Spike Milligan and friends. Sellers made superb films, including a satire of nuclear terror, *Dr. Strangelove* (discussed in Chapter 5). With John Antrobus, Milligan wrote and performed *The Bedsitting Room* (1963), a play about nuclear war survivors. Radioactivity mutates one character into a bed-sitting room, and he asks a doctor what to take for it. 'Thirty shillings a week – at a push you might get two quid,' answers Dr Kak (Milligan 1979: 23). Beginning in 1969, *Monty Python's Flying Circus* went beyond *Beyond the Fringe* and *The Goon Show*, with weekly television broadcasts featuring loony bureaucrats, singing lumberjacks, silly walks and other comic nonsense. Animation by Terry Gilliam added a more cartoonish sensibility to the mix.

Besides the televised satire of *Monty Python* and *Saturday Night Live* (which began in New York in 1970), television news broadcasts provided a format that was mimicked – along with people in the news – on programs such as *That Was the Week That Was, Have I Got News for You, Mock the Week, The Daily Show* and *The Colbert Report*. Viewers weary of grim daily reports from regular newscasts could find a more cheerful and sceptical perspective in these take-offs.

Tabloid journalism, Rupert Murdoch and his gossip-laden news empire received attention in *Pravda* (1985), a full-length satiric play by David Hare and Howard Brenton. Another satiric response to British gossip and people in the news in the 1980s took the form of rubbery, plasticine puppets televised on *Spitting Images*.

Off-camera, on small stages, other puppeteers have ably framed, distorted and ridiculed bad behaviour in a variety of geographic locations and historical periods. Most puppets fit in a suitcase or a trunk, which permits a large cast to travel cheaply (if someone carries the suitcase) and reach new audiences through touring. In the eighteenth century, the satiric potential of puppet shows was recognized by Jonathan Swift when he wrote that 'Punch roaring run, and running roar'd, / Revil'd all people in his jargon, / and sold the king of Spain a bargain... While, teasing all, by all he's teaz'd, / How well are the spectators pleas'd!' (Swift 1754: 256).

An influential American purveyor of puppetry, Peter Schumann, founded the Bread and Puppet Theatre company in New York in 1960, and since then his group has toured the world with shows that offer satire, historical commemorations and ritual. During the period of Vietnam War protests in the 1960s and 1970s, Bread and Puppet artists paraded along New York's streets with huge sculpted heads. One named Uncle Fatso looked like a malign, cigar-wielding Wall Street capitalist. Other puppets were papier maché images of wild animals, war victims, giant white cloth peace doves accompanied by a banner calling for a fight to prevent the end of the world. Bread and Puppet still annually presents mock-circuses with animal puppets at a farm in Glover, Vermont.

England's Welfare State, founded by John Fox in 1968, also created outdoor performances with puppets, pageantry and parade floats; its events like those of Bread and Puppet often took the form of processions against apocalypse and ceremonies for new mythologies with satire included. One could add to this honour roll puppetry created in Bali, Japan, India, China, Slovenia, France, other countries cited in Ilene Blumenthal's *Puppetry: A World History*. Nina Efimova's *Adventures of a Russian Puppet Theatre* also offers some vivid descriptions of satire on a small stage.

American Folly: Beyond Brecht and Cantinflas

Another small, portable stage featuring satire is that of the San Francisco Mime Troupe. Founded by R. G. Davis in 1959, widely seen and influential during its first few decades and still performing, the Mime Troupe has never been silent; its actors offer physical comedy, songs and topical dialogue. Drawing inspiration from protest rallies, Brecht, Fo, Marx, *commedia dell'arte,* musical comedy and melodrama, it responded to American folly with plays about military excursions abroad, the nation's bitter racial divide, CIA intrigue, controversial economic and immigration policies, and urban gentrification. Setting up its wooden platform stage in the parks of San Francisco, Berkeley, Oakland and other Californian cities, the ensemble charges no admission, only asks for donations after the performance, an age-old practice of popular theatre. Over the years a large number of writers and actors have collaborated collectively on Mime Troupe projects, among them writers Joan Holden, John O'Neal, Josh Kornbluth and Rotimi Agbabia, and directors Dan Chumley, Michael Sullivan and R.G. Davis. The titles of the plays preview their focus: *Eco Man, Frozen Wages, City for Sale, Walls, Oil and Water, The Minstrel Show, San Fran Scandals, Seeing Red, The Independent Female; or a Man Has His Pride.* They also performed plays by Brecht, Fo, Jarry and an adaptation of Goldoni (Figure 8).

Luiz Valdez left the Mime Troupe in 1965 to create his own touring ensemble, El Teatro Campesino, which performed short satiric plays about farm workers during their struggle to unionize on the West Coast. Initially the Latinx actors performed scenes outdoors on flatbed trucks for agricultural workers in consultation with union organizer Cesar Chavez of the United Farm Workers. Valdez and his company later created short and full-length plays about Mexican American life, including a satire on Chicano 'sellouts', *Los Vendidos* (1967), and an historically based musical *Zoot Suit* (1978).

Figure 8 *The San Francisco Mime Troupe performs* L'Amante Militaire, *San Francisco, 1967.*

The creativity of Valdez, inspired by Brecht, R. G. Davis and Mexican film comedian Cantinflas, set the stage for another satiric group, Culture Clash. Its program titled *A Bowl of Beings* (1991) featured a sketch in which Che Guevara turned up alive and well in Berkeley, California. A Berkeley activist named Chuy brings the revolutionary up to date on the pop culture and history he missed between the years of his death in 1967 and his resurrection in 1991: 'Commandante Che, these are crazy times. Communismo is on the way down, Starbucks Coffee is on the way up... you inspired a whole generation of yuppies [young urban professionals], and besides, you made a handsome silk-screen poster' (Montoya, Salinas and Siguenza 1998: 88–9). Satirists Richard Montoya, Ricardo Salinas and Herbert Siguenza, group founders, also bowed to (or winked at) Aristophanes in 1998 when they adapted *The Birds*. Their ensemble was particularly well received by cultural and geographical peers on the West Coast of the United States.

Over the past few decades, new plays exploring ethnic and racial identity have turned to satire as well as other theatre forms. Clichés and sentimentality about African-Americans were questioned in a series of parodic sketches by writer and director George C. Wolfe in *The Colored Museum* (1986). Wolfe's scenes included a take-off on the 'Mama on the Couch' play, a genre Lorraine Hansberry made almost sacred with *A Raisin in the Sun*. Hansberry's 1959 play about integration of housing in Chicago suffered another satiric response in Bruce Norris's *Clybourne Park* (2010), which shows a white family moving into a black community, reversing the original *Raisin* situation fifty years later. Langston Hughes in *Soul Gone Home* (1936), Amiri Baraka in *Jello* (1970), Suzan Lori-Parks in *The America Play* (1994) and Robert O'Hara in *Barbecue* (2015) also looked with humour at American culture, racism and racial stereotypes. Outside conventional theatres, on the street, in museums and art galleries, visual artists Adrian Piper, Dred Scott, Pope L. and David Hammons addressed African American concerns through inventive and satiric performance.

Theatrical satire also surfaced in short and hybrid forms of modern music and performance art. In the 1960s and 1970s, Fluxus events staged by John Cage, Yoko Ono, Joseph Beuys, Charlotte Moorman and Nam June Paik upended audience expectations with unpredictable mixes of media and humour. (They created serious pieces as well.) Cage, known for his experimental music compositions involving chance and silence, delivered a very funny solo performance in *Water Walk* (1959), a brief concert in which a tea kettle, a gong, a partially filled bathtub, a seltzer dispenser, randomly tuned radios and the composer's own precise movements (imbibing a mixed drink mid-performance) animated a comic sound score. Yoko Ono's miniature scenarios for performance asked her audience to turn into actors, with stage directions such as 'Keep laughing for a week' (the whole text of *Laugh Piece*) (Ono 1964). Some of these artists did not set out to create satire; but they achieved it by offering parodic and subversive departures from conventional concerts and art exhibits.

Most of the projects listed here originated in collaborative creation. American artists in the San Francisco Mime Troupe, Culture Clash, Bread and Puppet, El Teatro Campesino and Fluxus, and in England, artists in Welfare State, Belt and Braces Roadshow, Monstrous Regiment, 7:84 and the Joint Stock Company supported one another and developed an alternative culture, including a circuit of audiences friendlier and venues more open to their dissent than society at large.

Satire also crossed national borders through borrowings and adaptations by these groups. For example, in 1980 Belt and Braces adapted Dario Fo's *Accidental Death of an Anarchist* to acclaim in England, with actor Gavin Richards taking over the role Fo first played. What Fo called the 'farce of power', his satire of Italian police covering up their murder of an innocent man, acquired new language and local references in the Richards adaptation. Fo himself approved of this new work 'substituting for the violence practiced by the powers in Italy (the police, the judiciary, the economy of the banks and the multinationals) equally tragic and brutal facts from the recent history of England' (Fo 1980: iv). The benefits of collaboration on a satire that moved from Ireland to England, then visited France and the United States, will be looked at more closely in a history of Brendan Behan's *The Hostage*.

4

Joan Littlewood's Brendan Behan and the Making of Modern Satire

Throughout its history, stage satire has united theatre artists with their audience. From the tyranny of Cleon in ancient Athens to eighteenth-century censorship under Walpole, through the arrival of world war and authoritarianism in modern times, prominent individuals were ridiculed on stage while spectators sided with the satirists, briefly creating an alternative society controlled by artists, and happily so. Alternative societies were celebrated by characters in the plays, too. Even as they defied established laws and order, the highwaymen in *The Beggar's Opera*, the colonial adventurers in *Polly*, the thieves at the wedding in *The Threepenny Opera*, and oppressed slaves in *The Knights* found fellowship with one another that they could not find elsewhere. Gay's Macheath told members of his gang: 'we, Gentlemen, have still Honour enough to break through the Corruptions of the World', as if his men of the road were more reliable and honest than those higher in society (2013: 52). The audience at these plays found a comparable, if less larcenous, community by attending theatre. They could break through the corruptions of the world for a few hours too, with

oppositional laughter, songs and an agreeable assembly that
the staging of satire initiated.

Some modern theatre companies have created an alternative
world, a new, friendly community among themselves, in
rehearsals as well as performances. When actors, directors and
playwright share ideas in rehearsal discussions and test new
scenes in workshops, their collaborative creations become a
locus of free expression before their satire reaches the public.
A conventional theatre company, brought together for a
commercial production on Broadway or the West End, is likely
to be composed of actors who rehearse for three to six weeks.
The situation differed significantly for Joan Littlewood's
company, some of whose members worked together for years
prior to rehearsing Brendan Behan's *The Hostage* in 1958.
Littlewood's Theatre Workshop faced financial and artistic
challenges over the years; participants had disagreements, some
left, others arrived. A list of about 300 names, 'everybody who
was ever a member of Theatre Workshop' over three decades,
was compiled by Howard Goorney in his book on the company
(1981: 211–13). Artists who worked with Littlewood for a few
seasons would find more continuity from one production to
another, and more opportunity to voice their own views, than
most commercial productions offered. Part of that continuity
was provided by the director's continued interest in satiric,
politically engaged, ensemble-developed plays. *The Hostage*
became one of those plays. Before Littlewood produced it,
Behan's text about a young British soldier held captive in Dublin
by the IRA (Irish Republican Army) was simpler, sentimental,
more serious and written in Gaelic. The English version created
at Theatre Workshop not only doubled the play's length and
added half a dozen characters; under Littlewood's direction, in
collaboration with her actors and Brendan Behan, the play was
transformed into superb stage satire.

The rehearsal procedures Theatre Workshop followed when
working on *The Hostage* had precedents; but Littlewood's role
as director, and the innovations of other modern directors
working with ensembles, added something new to the history

of satire. When Aristophanes and John Gay wrote plays, the profession of stage director did not yet exist. It is likely Aristophanes directed his own work, and rehearsal of Gay's plays was probably conducted by the prompter and theatre manager at Lincoln's Inn Fields's. No detailed records of their rehearsal processes survive; but theatre history suggests that stage directors did not begin to exert considerable influence over acting ensembles until the Duke of Saxe-Meiningen worked with his troupe in nineteenth-century Germany. His practice of paying detailed attention to ensemble acting was followed in other prominent directorial efforts, Joan Littlewood's among them. She prepared actors for their roles with exercises, took time for improvisations and oversaw changes to the playwright's text. Behan's original Gaelic version of *The Hostage* and his translation of it provided a framework, a starting point for directorial insight and company rehearsals that enlarged the cast of characters and amount of dialogue. *The Quare Fellow*, an earlier play Behan wrote in English, needed no translation when Littlewood directed it in 1956; but its scenes of prison life underwent 'cutting and honing' 'with Behan's approval', and actor improvisations helped develop 'a realistic atmosphere' for the gallows humour (Holdsworth 2006: 27). That collaboration turned out to be a rehearsal of methods to which Behan and Littlewood's company would return when they produced *The Hostage*.

Joan Littlewood (1914–2002) created other satires and political plays earlier in her career when she collaborated with Ewan MacColl. Beginning in 1934, their work together drew on folklore, balladry, the political theatre practices of Meyerhold, Piscator and Brecht, and the comedy of Molière and Ben Jonson. In the late 1930s they staged a few anti-war satires – Aristophanes's *Lysistrata* and *The Good Soldier Schweik*, which Piscator and Brecht had developed earlier from Hasek's Czech novel. In 1940 Littlewood and MacColl created a Living Newspaper, *Last Edition*, inspired by the journalistically based plays of the Federal Theatre Project in the United States. After naming their group Theatre Workshop in 1945, they returned to some of the old themes – war, working-class opposition to tyranny and journalistic coverage of events – in new plays. In 1953 the company moved into the building that became its permanent home – Theatre Royal, Stratford, in London's East End. MacColl left at that time, but not before Littlewood had acquired from their partnership a working knowledge of modern theatre innovations: avant-garde, agit-prop (didactic and political theatre), musical and popular forms that contributed to her company's later creations. While set designer John Bury, actors Howard Goorney, Brian Murphy, Clive Barker, Murray Melvin, Eileen Kennally and Avis Bunnage, company manager Gerry Raffles and composer Lionel Bart may have shared Littlewood's preferences before joining her, she brought out the best in them when they collaborated on plays with working-class characters, satiric and politically engaged texts, an ensemble of actors willing to improvise and take chances. Playwrights also benefitted from these ensemble efforts.

Disputed Authorship

Molière and Jonson raised no objection to changes Theatre Workshop made in their plays; living writers were not always so cooperative. When Joan Littlewood produced the English premiere of *Mother Courage* in 1955, Brecht (who stayed in Berlin) insisted that the director herself had to play the title role. Not agreeing to this until late in the rehearsal process, she did not perform the role of Mother Courage to anyone's satisfaction. Behan's work on *The Hostage* also was vexing in 1958, when Littlewood sought to change and expand his translation. Writing about Theatre Workshop's collaboration with Behan, Alan Simpson says the playwright had some concerns that 'his enemies' might argue 'his plays had been "written for him"' (1978: 23). It would be more accurate to say that when Joan Littlewood rehearsed *The Hostage* with her actors, the author became part of a larger, more inclusive creative process, during which he was sometimes missing in action, out at a local pub, or at any rate not providing the expected new pages. The author's absence is mentioned within the play itself. After a song, Meg says to the lodging-house caretaker Pat: 'The author should have sung that one.' 'That's if the thing has an author,' replies Pat to his consort (Behan 1962a: 76).

However 'the thing' got written (which will be discussed), it became more of a satire in Theatre Workshop's rendering. The translated Gaelic text of *An Giall* (which means *The Hostage*) acquired new songs, jokes, bawdy scenes and more characters in the 1958 English version directed by Littlewood and changed further during its stage run. In the first scene of the Gaelic text, for example, Patrick and Kate (renamed Meg in later scripts) discuss bagpipe music – just the two of them (Behan 1987: 29). The first Theatre Workshop version opens with an Irish jig danced by many characters, and the first words spoken are a whore's warning to 'queers': 'Get off the stage, you dirty low things' (Behan 1959: 1). In a later edition, the first line spoken is Meg's: 'Thank God, that's over!' (Behan 1962a: 1). The opening lines spoken by a nameless whore and Meg humorously suggest that objectionable activity has just taken place; in both cases, that activity is a jig performed by prostitutes and homosexuals who did not appear in the Gaelic version. A two-character conversation in Gaelic gave way to an Irish fling featuring most of the cast as if to announce at the start: 'We're all in this together.'

That togetherness includes the audience, as characters directly address spectators from time to time in Theatre Workshop's version of the play. Towards the end of Act Two Leslie, the soldier held hostage, says that Brendan Behan is 'too anti-British'. An Irish Republican Army officer retorts Behan is too 'anti-Irish'. Leslie then turns to the audience and announces the author 'doesn't mind coming over here [England in 1958–9] and taking your money', citing this as proof of the playwright's willingness to sell out. Before spectators can say anything, the disagreement escalates, flags of three nations are unfurled, the entire cast argues identity and politics, and 'the fight breaks up into a wild dance' (Behan 1962a: 76–7). No one, including spectators, is left out of the riotous scene, which is far more inclusive than the Gaelic version. In fact, Act Two of the Gaelic script has none of the scene just described.

Theatre Workshop's expansive ensemble rendering of the play, distinctive in its own right, also serves as an outstanding example of post-war collaboration by a group of theatre artists. Other British, American, European and Asian theatre directors employed experimental collaborative processes in the 1960s and 1970s. They were not necessarily following the example Theatre Workshop set in 1958, or in 1963 with *Oh What a Lovely War*. But in decades that followed *The Hostage*, the increased involvement of directors and acting ensembles in the shaping of play texts could be seen in the work of groups led by Tadeusz Kantor, Peter Brook, Ariane Mnouchkine, William Gaskill, Max Stafford-Clark, John McGrath, Joe Chaikin, Judith Malina, Julian Beck, Jerzy Grotowski, Anne Bogart, Andrei Serban and Tadashi Suzuki. A playwright (if there was one) working with any of these companies was no longer the primary or only source of a performance text. Brecht at the Berliner Ensemble with his dramaturgs and assistant directors in the early 1950s, and Artaud in his book *The Theatre and Its Double* provided models for these collaborative practices too. Words were treated as one component of an art incorporating the input of actors, designers, music composers and choreographers. Joan Littlewood's approach to plays was by no means the only one to explore the benefits of collective theatre creation led by a stage director; but she led her company towards satire more often than the other directors listed here. Theatre Workshop's production of *The Hostage* in 1958 was consonant with, and anticipatory of, other ensemble creations of satiric plays such as Caryl Churchill's *Cloud Nine* (1979), developed with London's Joint Stock Company; Dario Fo's *Accidental Death of an Anarchist* (1970) and other plays he created with La Comune, an Italian *collettivo teatrale* (theatre collective); and company works by the San Francisco Mime Troupe, Monstrous Regiment, 7:84, Belt and Braces Roadshow in the 1960s, 1970s and later. Performers in some of the groups (particularly Littlewood's, Mnouchkine's, Fo's and the Mime Troupe's) also worked with Italian *commedia dell'arte* scenarios and acting exercises that call for improvisation. *Commedia* plays and their popular comedy routines (*lazzi*) were not credited to a single author.

Around the same time these modern theatres collectively developed plays, a theory about 'the death of the author' was articulated by Michel Foucault, who contended that texts were subject to a loss or dispersion of singular authorial voice (Foucault 1977: 121, 128). Foucault's suggestion that authors formerly were expected to have a 'particular point of view', but may no longer have one, is affirmed with humour in *The Hostage* when the characters discuss their playwright:

Meg: Ah, he'd sell his country for a pint.
Pat: And put up his hands and thank the Almighty God that he had a country to sell.
Soldier: Author, author.
Monsewer: Author!
Pat: He might as well show up; it's his only bleeding chance of getting a curtain call.

(Behan 1959: 64–5)

Once in a while Behan sat in the audience and took a curtain call; but most nights the author's 'point of view' in *The Hostage* was expressed by multiple characters who disagreed about the past and future of Ireland, as well as their play's authorship.

Another Irish writer, Sean O'Casey, wanted to see more of Behan and less of Littlewood. In a letter sent to Alan Simpson he objected that 'Miss L' 'tampered' with the plays of Brendan Behan and Shelagh Delaney (author of *A Taste of Honey*). 'She may have improved them, but the point with me is that, even so, they ceased to be the work of the playwrights, and became the

Figure 9 *Joan Littlewood and Brendan Behan, 1960.*

work of J. Littlewood' (O'Casey quoted by Simpson 1978: 21).
To which objections Littlewood might have responded with
a statement (one she wrote, but not in answer to O'Casey):
'Nobody ever really wrote on their own. Aristophanes or Ben

Jonson or Brecht. Theatre is collaborative' (quoted in Schafer 1999: 161). It is interesting that she named three authors of satire here, all three far from 'nobody'. Littlewood worked on texts by all three before producing *The Hostage*.

She once declared, 'I do not believe in the supremacy of the director, designer, actor or even of the writer. It is through collaboration that this knockabout art of theatre survives and kicks. It was true at The Globe, The Curtain, The Crown, and in the "illustrious theatre" of Moliere and it can work here, today' (1965: 133). One corollary of this disbelief is that Littlewood should not be singled out for praise too often. Although her accomplishments were admired by Charles Marowitz, he declined to 'join that chorus which chants: we need more Joan Littlewoods. What England needs is more companies as well-fibred and resilient as Theatre Workshop was in its heyday... the growth of living ensembles instead of the useless fragmentation of the present one-shot, commercial system' (1965: 233) (Figure 10).

Figure 10 *Joan Littlewood rehearses* The Hostage.

While *The Hostage* was devised through collaboration, and reflects that process in its dialogue, it shares with the satires of Gay and Aristophanes a proclivity for songs, topical references and ridicule of authority figures. Behan's play differs from the satires of earlier periods insofar as he and Littlewood drew on popular entertainment forms that didn't exist in ancient Athens or Gay's London: namely, music hall, melodrama and the modern panto (pantomime). Playwright David Edgar inadvertently called attention to these influences when he argued Theatre Workshop 'employed forms actually peripheral to the urban British working class', and director John McGrath responded that 'music hall, variety' and similar entertainment forms were not at all 'peripheral to the urban working class' or Behan's play. McGrath recalled:

> By some strange chance I happened to be at the dress rehearsal of *The Hostage*, with Brendan Behan shouting friendly drunken abuse at the actors through the second half, and them giving him back as good as they got, and Joan charging around muttering, unable to sit still for very long. What was happening on the stage, in the pub down Angel Lane, in the street outside the door, all seemed to be of a piece in the same universe. ... they were telling [a story] the way the working class saw it, and in a way that the working class could enjoy, and what is more, *did* enjoy.
>
> (McGrath 1981: 46, 48)

From McGrath's perspective, Behan became a contributor to an ongoing, extended repertory of plays fit for a working-class audience. *The Hostage* was just as suitable for that as a variety show and other popular entertainments. The play's mix of comic patter, self-reflective asides, Irish ballads and topical satire was a kind of variety show, a medley (one of the original meanings of 'satire' or *satura*). Behan came up with a novel description of this mixed form when he called *The Hostage* an 'uproarious tragedy' (Brien 1982: 264).

Pure Behan?

The play's mixture of ingredients made it difficult for critic Kenneth Tynan to classify the work when he first saw it. He wrote, 'conventional terminology is totally inept to describe the uses to which Mr. Behan and his director, Joan Littlewood, are trying to put the theatre. The old pigeon-holes will no longer serve.' Then Tynan ignored his own advice and resorted to an old pigeon-hole by declaring, '*The Hostage* is a Commedia dell-Arte production.' After seeing *The Hostage* again when it moved to the West End, Tynan amended his earlier verdict and wrote that the play 'is a babble of styles, devoid of form yet full of attack – *Hellz-a-Poppin,* you might say, with a point of view' (1961: 219, 235). His reference to *Hellz-a-Poppin* recalls earlier entertainments that opened in New York under the direction of two comedians, Ole Olsen and Chic Johnson. The creators of Broadway's *Hellzapoppin* series drew on their experiences in vaudeville, and put together evenings of songs, dances, and comedy sketches.

Ireland's history and its past theatre also provided inspiration for Behan's work. Pat, the lodging-house caretaker in *The Hostage*, displays the relaxed, friendly assurance of a storyteller versed in tales of Ireland's civil war heroes and the poetry of folk ballads. His language and character are not so far removed from those of men in plays by Sean O'Casey and John Millington Synge, both influenced by Irish folklore and the country's troubles. Born in Dublin, Behan (1923–64) was attracted at a young age to IRA activity, some of which led him to serve prison sentences in Borstal and Mountjoy. He later reflected on prison life in the book *Borstal Boy* and his full-length play, *The Quare Fellow*, whose title character is sentenced to hang. Two leading Dublin theatres, the Abbey and the Gate, rejected that play. First produced in 1954 by the Pike Theatre, a small Dublin house, *The Quare Fellow* was then staged at Theatre Workshop in 1956.

In 1958 when Tynan saw *The Hostage*, praised it and
connected the play to Italian *commedia*, the critic had an
intriguing reservation. He wrote that one cannot 'be sure how
much of the dialogue is pure Behan and how much is gifted
embroidery; for the whole production sounds spontaneous,
a communal achievement based on Miss Littlewood's idea of
theatre as a place where people talk to people, not actors to
audiences' (1961: 220). Tynan was right to ask whether the
play is 'pure Behan' or 'a communal achievement'. By the
time Joan Littlewood and her associates opened *The Hostage*,
it had lost its Gaelic title and gained many other features.
After the Gaelic premiere at Damer Hall, Dublin, on 16
June 1958, the English-language version opened at Theatre
Workshop on 14 October 1958, subsequently moved to the
Théâtre des Nations festival in Paris (April 1959), and then to
Wyndham's Theatre on London's West End (June 1959). The
'embroidered' and enlarged text seen by Tynan was developed
between August and October of 1958. Behan began work on
the English translation in August, and the script was revised
during ensemble rehearsals. Some changes did not begin in
written form, but with songs and stories the writer in person
shared with the actors. Colbert Kearney credits Behan with
giving Littlewood 'the basis of a workshop play rather than a
script in the traditional sense' (Kearny quoted by Mac Craith
2019: 128).

Like the hostage in his play, Behan himself was held captive
one night during the rehearsal period. Littlewood and her
associates, particularly Gerry Raffles, had pressed the author
to deliver additional material, and one evening Raffles sat the
author down at a desk, pointed a gun at Behan and ordered
him to write; that too constitutes a kind of collaboration.
When not writing under the gun, but gregariously sharing
songs, anecdotes, impersonations with actors and director,
Behan provided 'material which could be incorporated into
the script', a phrase from Howard Goorney that suggests the
author gave actors and director lines or lyrics before they
were written down (Goorney 1981: 110). Records of these

transactions are sketchy and not necessarily accurate, but different sources agree Behan's script advanced through his interaction with others during the rehearsal period. Writing about the production in her autobiography, *Joan's Book*, Littlewood never mentions the three-act Irish version of the play that preceded Theatre Workshop's text. She recalls: 'The Saturday before we were due to open, we still had no Act Three... How to finish the story? Inspiration, a police raid. It was the only way out. Ad lib at first' (1994: 529).

That they 'had no Act Three' a week before opening is debatable. Alan Simpson, who produced some of Behan's plays and saw different drafts of *The Hostage*, writes that from the beginning the play had three acts, but 'the Irish text is very short, especially in Act Three'. The published text of *An Giall* has three acts (Behan 1987: 65–74). Perhaps Littlewood refers only to the incomplete English translation she had at the time. Simpson confirms that Littlewood's production introduced to the play a number of new characters, Mulleady, a 'decaying Civil Servant', and Miss Gilchrist, an evangelical social worker, both of whom 'show signs... of the improvisation of English actors and the farcical talents of Mr. Behan himself. The other extra characters seem to have evolved from Ropeen, Colette, the Rat, Sod, Scholars and Bobo, who in the Irish text are mentioned as residents in the establishment (which is called "The Hole") but do not actually appear on stage' (Simpson in Behan 1978: 19–20). Also added were a number of direct addresses to the audience from Pat, Meg, Gilchrist and Leslie. These brief speeches break the situational frame, but they are casually introduced, a far cry from the long *parabases* delivered in Aristophanes's plays; they come closer to the kind of speech a panto actor or a Brecht character would make explaining his or her situation to spectators.

In his writing for the stage Behan also may have drawn on his panto experiences, which he recalled in a column he wrote for *The Irish Press*. '"Fun with vulgarity" was the motto of our pantomime,' he bragged in the article that discussed panto songs, a stage joke about Mountjoy Prison, and the Gaelic name of an actress (Behan 1963: 140–1). His enthusiasm for pantomime also could account in part for Behan's attraction to Joan Littlewood's stage, where fun and music, if not vulgarity, were primary ingredients. Dierdre McMahon suggests that the music hall entertainments and Victorian melodramas Behan saw at his uncle P. J. Bourke's theatre influenced the composition of *The Hostage*. 'He adopts stock ingredients of melodrama and music hall only to subvert them; he raises expectation of generic convention only to interrupt it with parody and farce' (McMahon 2019: 64, 67).

After completing *The Hostage* and reflecting on its journey from Gaelic to English, Behan confessed:

> I wrote the play very quickly – in about twelve days or so. I wrote it in Irish and it was first put on in Irish in Dublin. I saw the rehearsal of this version and while I admire the producer, Frank Dermody tremendously, his idea of a play is not my idea of a play. He's of the school of Abbey Theatre naturalism of which I'm not a pupil. Joan Littlewood, I found, suited my requirements exactly. She has the same views on the theatre that I have, which is that the music hall is the thing to aim for to amuse people and any time they get bored, divert them with a song or a dance. (1962b: 17)

While *The Hostage* was removed from naturalism in its Theatre Workshop staging, the resulting production admirably exemplified another form of theatre. For all its irregularities or departures from conventional pigeon-holes, for all its debt to music hall, panto, *commedia* and melodrama, the play became an outstanding model of modern stage satire. Modern in its collaborative creation, but traditional in meeting criteria for stage satire proposed centuries earlier by Jonathan Swift when, responding to John Gay's play, he wrote, 'although some things are too serious, solemn, or sacred to be turned into ridicule, yet the abuses of them are certainly not, since it is allowed that corruption in religion, politics and law, may be proper topics for this kind of satire' (Swift 1730: 21).

In the course of having characters debunk one another's religion, politics and law as they discuss loyalty to Ireland, gossip about the royal family, nostalgically recall IRA history and their role in it, Behan ridicules long-lasting nationalism, militarism, religious fervour, beliefs and causes that motivate the hostage-taking. The kidnapping of a British soldier is not inherently comic; admirers of the earlier Gaelic version of *The Hostage* saw more tender romance and melodrama in the story than Theatre Workshop's production offered. Theatre Royal, Stratford's enlarged, motley crew of characters disrupted the IRA's dead serious operation with considerable distraction, bawdiness and humour, and turned a small tragedy, *An Giall*, into satire.

What's Civil about a Civil War?

As the Theatre Workshop production added new songs and shenanigans to Behan's first draft, the play also acquired more topical references to Ireland, England and the conflict between them. One change Richard Wall noticed in Theatre Workshop's revision of the Gaelic text was that 'the general attitude of the Irish toward Leslie [the hostage] and the English is much more hostile' (Behan 1987: 17). In Act Two characters report that a march of support for the IRA prisoner held in Belfast included banners reading: 'England, the hangman of thousands. In Ireland, in Kenya, in Cyprus' and 'Another victim for occupied Ireland'. Leslie steps towards the audience after this and explains to them that the 'bloke in the Belfast Jail' is 'going to be topped tomorrow morning' without yet knowing that he may be executed in reprisal (1962a: 51–2). He learns of his own possible execution near the end of Act Two, and once the hostage realizes no one in the room will help him escape, the captive soldier unleashes a round of invective against nonwhites and the Irish. He starts his own civil war, becomes an offensive, nativist Englishman as he sings:

I am a happy English lad, I love my royal-ty...
I love my dear old Notting Hill, wherever I may roam.
But I wish the Irish and the niggers and the wogs,
Were kicked out and sent back home.

(1962a: 78)

His harsh attack on 'foreigners' here may be undercut visually, shown to be a lonely man's anxious response to abandonment and a death threat. Rage and unhappiness can be read (or heard) between the lines. His stunning display of prejudice may carry over into Act Three and undermine Leslie's protestations of innocence. Lashing out, lying about being happy, he becomes a hostage to his own prejudices with the song that closes Act Two. No one is going to rescue this angry young man. An earlier song lyric, 'no one loves you like yourself', would be appropriate here too, but not very funny. The silence that follows the song (because Act Two is over) makes Leslie's isolation quite evident. In other scenes he is not alone; residents in the house – Teresa, Gilchrist, the gay men – befriend the prisoner, take his side, flirt with him. He is a wanted man in every sense.

Except for a few outbursts of racism, sexism and violence (none endorsed by the author), Behan's play looks with genial humour at the hostage and others of differing religious, political and sexual persuasions. The author embraces them all with varying degrees of affection, even when mocking their faults. But fault he finds; this is after all a satire. Things serious, solemn and sacred are subjected to derision, and that includes the Irish Republican Army. Placed among sex workers and housekeepers who do not share their dedication to the cause, the IRA men find their mission obstructed, questioned, undermined. When the play was first performed in the late 1950s, its references to civil war were more than history notes. The Irish Republican Army was still conducting raids in Northern Ireland. Pat declares, 'This is nineteen fifty-eight, and the days of the heroes is over this thirty-five years past... The I.R.A. and the War of Independence are...

as dead as the Charleston' (1959: 2). But Monsewer, an IRA veteran who welcomes the kidnappers into his house, argues, 'there are still young men willing and ready to go out and die for Ireland' (Behan 1959: 34). Despite its many comic moments, or through them, the play voices serious concerns about colonial occupation by military force and addresses the conditions that led to violent heroics in Ireland before and after the play's London production. Behan spent several years in prison (1939–41) for his possession of explosives, several more (1942–6) for firing a gun at a detective in Dublin; and while his play hardly propagandizes on behalf of the IRA, it never fully renounces Republican Army practices either. The night Theatre Workshop opened *The Quare Fellow* in 1956, its audience included 'three I.R.A. men who had been barred from the country, more than fifteen recognized leaders of the Republican Movement, men whose prison sentences totaled three hundred years', according to Howard Goorney (1981: 105). If a few of those men got past the bar again and returned to Theatre Workshop for *The Hostage,* they would have seen comic versions of themselves or their friends on stage. Behan was talking about them when Pat, speaking of his years in prison for IRA activity, asks what 'the worst thing is' about prison and answers, 'The other Irish patriots in along with you... There'd be a split straight away' (Behan 1962a: 51). A little like Cleon, the general who watched himself mocked by *The Knights*, IRA veterans and sympathizers could see their counterparts satirized at Theatre Royal, Stratford in 1958.

Some English men and women attended, too, no doubt; but the house had room for only 460 spectators (Thomas 2006). The limited seating capacity did not prevent *The Hostage* from reaching a large audience; favourable press, a move to London's West End and performances in Paris and New York made it internationally popular. Most of the spectators were not IRA members, but anyone with incipient anti-authoritarian tendencies could enjoy Behan's mockery of an officious Irish patriot known only as 'Officer'. An unbending, uncompromising authority figure, the Officer becomes Pat's straight man, with his serious demeanour undermined as soon as he arrives. Teresa informs Pat that the Officer wears two badges. One badge claims he speaks only Irish, but his first lines and most others are English. The second badge says the Officer doesn't drink. 'That means he's a higher officer,' deduces Pat. Stage directions describe the official as 'a thin-faced fanatic in a trench coat and black beret' who 'is really a schoolmaster'; it's not a flattering picture. IRA enabler Monsewer, said to have been a rebel army general, also wins no compliments from Behan's stage directions, which indicate the bagpipe player 'isn't right in the head', 'lives in a world of his own, peopled by heroes and enemies', and the noise from his bagpipes 'is terrible' (1962a: 1, 6).

Lines suggesting that the IRA is obsolete give the play itself a built-in defence against obsolescence; some of its characters are holdovers from the past trying to live in the present. While events are set in 1958, the play also revels in civil war history, and Behan's look back is hardly reverential. The Officer might as well be speaking to the playwright when he warns Pat: 'This is no laughing matter, you idiot.' Pat responds, 'there are two sorts of gunmen, the earnest, religious-minded ones, like you and the laughing boys' (1962a: 50). If he was either type, Behan was a laughing boy; he finds humour in Irish Republican Army representatives and his country's history. By the time he wrote the play, he was far more of a storyteller and entertainer than a gunman.

Judging from the play's ridicule of Monsewer and other IRA stalwarts, Behan was not so keen on rebels dying for Ireland or killing for it in late 1950s. The hostage is accidentally smothered and his loss immediately lamented in *An Giall*. In the Theatre Workshop version Leslie Williams is shot during a raid. The play's stage directions do not reveal who shot the lad; they simply say: 'Shots. Soldier falls' (1959: 91) and 'a deafening blast of gunfire and he drops' (1962a: 107). According to the 1962 text's stage directions, the lodger Mulleady 'has informed on Pat and Monsewer and has brought the police in to rescue Leslie' after inviting the house's homosexuals into his scheme, and the Russian in the house 'has been a police spy all along' (1962a: 103–4). The details of this conspiracy would be hard to detect in the panic and confusion of the raid, during which the Russian says nothing, the piano 'is playing sinisterly', Leslie runs around in search of an exit, and two nuns who enter the room turn out to be IRA men in disguise. The scene of the shooting is more farce than tragedy, or both at once, and in this context Leslie's arising from the dead is not a miracle, only another departure from stage conventions of realism.

From 'Naturalistic Tragedy' to 'Musical Extravaganza'

Before the shooting of the British soldier can be called a tragedy, though not before Teresa keens for her lost love, the sense of loss is reduced considerably in Theatre Workshop's version. Leslie removes the nun's cloak placed over his corpse, slowly stands up and sings: 'The bells of hell / Go ting-a-ling-a-ling / For you but not for me. / Oh death where is thy / Sting-a-ling-a-ling / Or grave thy victory?' (1962a: 108). The entire cast joins him for the closing lines, a company united in its denial of death's sting. The same lyrics turned up five years later in *Oh What a Lovely War*, which suggests Littlewood and company enjoyed reviving soldiers' songs as well as soldiers.

The ensemble's singing, particularly the refrain asking 'death, where is thy sting-a-ling-a-ling', turns what could be a tragic scene into comic operetta. Prescribing no solution to Ireland's troubles, the play instead confirms Robert Leach's view that Theatre Workshop 'did not so much confront the reality of the time as subvert it and hold it up to ridicule' (2006: 151). Even death is mocked. With its comic patter, songs and farcical action *The Hostage* lets alleged enemies spend some time together, fall in love, die and come back to life in a world very different from the one outside the theatre.

Then again, the world was not so different from Behan's play, according to the playwright. His plot was inspired by actual events. Talking about the play's origins in *Brendan Behan's Island*, the author said that Nelson Street in Dublin was

> where I happened to set the scene of *The Hostage*. Most of the incidents in that play were taken from life though, needless to say, I fiddled around a lot with them – catch me leaving anything unembroidered. The incident of the British Tommy occurred actually in Belfast but, in real life, I'm happy to say, he wasn't shot. As a matter of fact, he said later that he spent the best four days of his life in the hands of the I.R.A. He was captured at a place called Bellykinlar Camp in County Down. He wasn't taken as a hostage at all but he'd been around by accident when the I.R.A. were raiding the place for arms, so they brought him home with them for a while.
>
> (Behan 1962b: 14)

Behan underestimates his own comic achievement; when he and Littlewood 'fiddled around' with events they became more theatrical, more musical, more satirical. Perhaps he refers here only to his first draft, the Gaelic version which has been described as a 'naturalistic tragedy' 'transmuted into a musical extravaganza' by the time it opened on Theatre Workshop's stage (Mac Craith 2019: 129). Ulick O'Connor preferred the first production and complained that the play 'in the West End and Paris... is a blown-up hotch-potch compared with the original which is a small masterpiece and the best thing Behan wrote for the theatre' (O'Connor quoted by Mac Craith 2019: 129). Admittedly the Theatre Workshop version, which could be called a larger masterpiece, was not composed solely by Behan, and in that sense may not be the best thing *he* wrote. But the longer version includes many welcome additions if one is looking for satire rather than tragedy. Behan himself welcomed the additions according to Littlewood, who reports that when the author saw all the parts of the English production 'put together for the first time' he said, 'I like the Littlewood bits, too' (Littlewood 1994: 537).

Defenders of Behan's Gaelic draft of *The Hostage* don't care much for the Anglo-Irish language version, or the additional jokes, anecdotes and songs that make the play more of satire and less of a tragedy. The Gaelic text ends with Teresa's lament for the dead soldier, no resurrection or song. And while the revised play cannot accurately be called a 'musical extravaganza' due to all the speeches delivered between songs, it should be noted that a piano player named Kate resides in the ramshackle house, always ready for a signal to begin the next number.

'Death-defying' with its resurrection of the hostage, Theatre Workshop's satire is also life-affirming as the young, lonely Belfast soldier courts Teresa when his guards leave them alone. Leslie asks to hear Teresa's life story, and she recalls childhood life in a convent. Her talk about a procession of the Blessed Virgin seems out of place in a house full of sex workers. 'Blessed who?' asks her Protestant listener, Leslie (1962a: 68). But Teresa is not so innocent herself, once a whirlwind musical romance starts. The couple sings a duet promising each other gifts if they marry. In the last line of the song, Leslie declares: 'But first I think that we should see / If we fit each other.' Teresa turns to the audience and asks: 'Shall we?' soliciting raucous applause and cheers before the couple runs to a bed and lights black out (1962a: 71). Representatives of Ireland's separated, warring halves are comically, licentiously united. By contrast, the romance in *An Giall* is quite chaste. When Teresa dances to radio music with Leslie Williams, she receives her 'first serious kiss' and he admits, 'Seriously, Teresa, I haven't any girl' (1987: 60). It's too serious for satire.

Toying with Apocalypse

Behan and Littlewood gave the hostage's captivity and romance considerable attention; but they enlarged the scope of their satire beyond these actions by adding brief, comic takes on other topics from moon exploration to World War III. Violence in Ireland becomes, in this context, a small sample of global dangers. Pat jovially acknowledges the situation: 'The H-Bomb. It's such a big bomb it's got me scared of the little bombs. The I.R.A. is out of date' (1962a: 5). Considering men far away from Dublin in an age of space exploration, bedroom evangelist Miss Gilchrist sings a hymn with the refrain: 'Don't muck about with the moon.' *The Hostage* also takes swipes at men and women who held prominent positions in the late 1950s. Today an audience might need a programme glossary to appreciate the references to British Prime Minister Harold Macmillan, American Secretary of State John Foster Dulles, film star Diana Dorn, Irish Prime Minister Eamon de Valera, rock singer Peter Townsend, boating enthusiast Uffa Fox and the Special Powers Act. Topical references changed during the play's extended run. When *The Hostage* moved to Broadway, according to producer Caroline Swann, 'daily newspapers were required reading by the actors who would insert references about current events every night. They warmed up before each performance by reading aloud choice bits from the newspapers' (1982: 164).

While a few of the play's topical speeches may benefit from nightly changes, its three-act structure moves plot and subplot forward sensibly, sequentially, distracted but not stopped by scripted disruptions. Preparations for the hostage's arrival lead to his entry, his romance, his death and sudden revival. Each act begins with a group of characters onstage before shifting to more private exchanges, and each act ends with a song. Songs that end Acts One and Three bring the entire company together and deny differences among the characters.

The prisoner's song at the end of Act One begins after he is pushed around by IRA soldiers during a dance reel. Leslie tells the Officer he likes the dancing and doesn't want it to stop. The Officer answers, 'Keep your mouth shut, and get up there,' after which the hostage defiantly halts and sings: 'There's no place on earth like the world, / There's no place wherever you be' (1962a: 40).

As other characters on stage join in, including Leslie's captors, a musical truce temporarily ends the hostility. Instead of the H-bomb that their lyrics predict will fuse the north and south poles, music unites them. At the same time, the lyrics suggest it may be better to keep the poles separated and not have a nuclear war. Toying with apocalypse, predicting and denigrating nuclear war, Act One concludes much as it began, with a community united by satire, music and rehearsed cooperation.

Not Grace Kelly

Although the hostage is alone, almost abandoned at the end of Act Two, Leslie is rarely deprived of company in other scenes. Teresa tries to comfort him. Miss Gilchrist finds him attractive. The homosexuals and whores in the house also take his side. After Leslie protests his innocence, saying he hasn't poked his nose into political affairs and never knew 'anything about Ireland or Cyprus or Kenya or Jordan or any of those places', and he should not be executed, Princess Grace and the whores in the house defend him: 'It's not his fault' (1959: 81). The gay men (including Mulleady, who turns out to be bisexual) have cause to sympathize with the hostage, as they too have been persecuted in Ireland – for being gay. Just as proud and defiant in their identity as Leslie was in his at the end of Act Two, Princess Grace and friends sing lyrics announcing, 'We're here because we're queer' (1962a: 97). Laws in the 1950s made homosexual activity a crime in both England and Ireland; punishment of offenders did not relent until 1967 in England, 1993 in Ireland. It may be a cliché to say that politics makes strange bedfellows; but the defence of Leslie by queer men in 1958 is not so strange, given that they were all unwelcome in Dublin. Mulleady leads the other gay men through a plan to rescue the political prisoner; the plan fails, but for a few minutes Leslie has new allies.

Behan introduced homosexual characters and a 'coloured' man to his play's mix at a time such men were not often seen on stage or openly 'queer' there, particularly not in the company of Irish rebels. The inclusion of Rio Rita, described as 'a homosexual navvy', and 'his coloured boyfriend', Princess Grace, made the play more than a satiric attack on military discipline, warfare and racism. (Grace Kelly, a famous Princess at the time, is not mentioned, only gently mocked by the partial use of her name.)

Around the same time he wrote *An Giall*, Behan looked at homosexuality among prison inmates in his book *Borstal Boy*. Homosexual life becomes freer and more affirmatively comic in *The Hostage*, as the queers come out in public and sing. Their house would be a liberated zone enjoying a variety of sexual escapades if it did not also hold a prisoner.

Defiance of sexual conventions in the play overlaps defiance of other attempts at social control. As the situation becomes comically anarchic, the Officer, also known as 'the laddie from headquarters', speaks of 'the need for discipline'. Pat mocks the IRA officer's seriousness with a playfulness that might be called disorderly conduct. 'Have you got the place well covered, sir?' he asks. The Officer responds, 'I have indeed. Why?' 'I think it's going to rain,' answers Pat. 'No more tomfoolery, please,' responds the Officer (1962a: 66). But tomfoolery is the order of the day. No character fully commands the situation, though a number of them quixotically try to take charge.

Laws governing sexual conduct have changed since 1958, but sexual discrimination and variations of the racism, militarism and nativism Behan derisively portrayed are still very much alive, and most references to these practices in *The Hostage* retain their bite. After Monsewer sings nativist lyrics praising colonial occupation and thanking 'God that we are white, / And better still are English', Pat acknowledges audience discomfort at the song's conclusion: 'Well, that's brought the show to a standstill' (1962a: 65). Monsewer represents a generation older and more culturally conservative than most residents in the rooming house, and he is dismissed as an idiot after his song. The hostage displays similar prejudice, as noted earlier, although he's on the opposite side in the war. Behan counters both men's bias with scenes of tolerance and reconciliation. As deviser of the plot, he could be regarded as an IRA ally; he helps the kidnappers pursue a peaceful trade of prisoners. But he also tacitly shows the limits of theatrical satire, which can oppose prejudice and violence but not stop it. The Dublin hostage and the boy held in Belfast Jail both die.

Caryl Churchill's Ghost

Caryl Churchill also introduces a soldier killed in Belfast in *Cloud Nine* (1979). The scene is not satiric, but other parts of her play are. The dead soldier appears briefly as a ghost in Act Two. Creating the play in collaboration with the ensemble of London's Joint Stock Company, Churchill in her own way continued procedures of playwriting and political reference that Littlewood and Behan developed in *The Hostage*. Both plays show a 'parallel between colonial and sexual oppression', as Churchill said of her work (Churchill 1985: 245). In *Cloud Nine* the Belfast soldier's thwarted sexual drive surfaces in foul language. Bill, the ghost of an occupying army's troops, the afterlife of British colonialism, is asked if he has come back to London to tell his sister something. He answers: 'No, I've come for a fuck. That was the worst thing in the fucking army. Never fucking let out. Can't fucking talk to the Irish girls. Fucking bored out of my fucking head' (1985: 310–11). In *The Hostage*, Leslie gets to talk and make love to an Irish girl in a temporary cessation of hostilities. Two decades later, the women in Churchill's *Cloud Nine* are more likely to love one another than a man in their liberated, feminist and lesbian world. Lin, the soldier's sister, responds with compassion to his complaint by saying, 'I miss you. Bill', and then the ghost departs.

The first act of Churchill's play, set in British colonial Africa of 1879, ridicules Victorian hypocrisy, racism and patriarchy. Act Two, set in London a century later, mixes satire with seriousness as it responds to prejudices held by English men and women in 1979. Although the scene with the soldier's ghost is grim, elsewhere in Act Two patriarchy and male chauvinism take quite a ribbing when self-assured Martin tells his wife's mother, Betty, that he is 'writing a novel about women from the women's point of view'. Unaware of how absurd and arrogant his ambition sounds, Martin's overreaching also leads him to tell his wife, Victoria, that his 'one aim is to give you pleasure. My one aim is to give you rolling orgasms like I do other women. So why the hell don't you have them?' (1985: 300–2). Perhaps if Aristophanes had been a woman writing in 1979, this is the language and humour we would hear.

Not all satire requires ensemble collaboration, of course; but like Behan's writing for Littlewood, Churchill's workshop with Joint Stock and director Max Stafford-Clark enabled actors to join in the genesis of their roles, to explore sexual and political repression and emerge with some satire. The process of *Cloud Nine*'s creation led to cross-gender casting and role doubling that expressed the company's concerns with race and gender in surprisingly comic ways at times. This and other innovative Churchill plays, notably *Serious Money*, *Far Away* and *The Escape*, offer satire combined with surreal and apocalyptic visions of social discord. One future prospect for new plays indicated by Churchill's writing as well as Behan's is the inclusion of satire in a mixed form such as 'uproarious tragedy' or 'tragicomedy'. Plays by both writers offer scenes of a divided community in crisis, devised by a cooperative community of theatre artists.

More crises and another mixture of forms – documentary drama, clowning and music hall comedy – appear in *Oh What a Lovely War*, first performed by Theatre Workshop in 1963. This play like *The Hostage* questioned the armed defence of national interests. Militarism from 1914 to 1918 was mocked and lamented; like its ironically cheerful play title, the war documented onstage did not turn out to be so lovely. Satire and dead seriousness alternated as troops underwent a shelling, then a news panel projection reported a British loss of 60,000 men on the first day of a battle on the Somme, then strains of 'Rule, Britannia' gave way to two drunken soldiers singing:

> I don't want to be a soldier,
> I don't want to go to war,
> I'd rather stay at home,
> Around the streets to roam,
> And live on the earnings of a lady typist.
>
> (Theatre Workshop 1965: 70, 77)

Near the conclusion of these scenes, a character wondered if the war might continue until 1964. It did, insofar as the play kept the First World War's story alive in 1964 and later. It moved from the East End to the West End, Paris and New York, then enjoyed afterlife in a film starring famous British actors (directed by Richard Attenborough), quite different from the play but bearing the original title.

Under Littlewood's direction Theatre Workshop first developed the play by using First World War songs, photographs, historical accounts and memoirs as source material, and drew on the conventions and performance history of once popular Pierrot shows. Performers dressed like Pierrot clowns in loose white blouses with wide sleeves, ruffled collars, fool's caps. Their jolly festivity suitable for a music hall gave way to men in military clothing planning battles and reading casualty reports, with photographs of war projected on a screen. Brian Murphy, an actor in the original production, said that the 'cast were completely involved in building up the script. We improvised a lot of different scenes, read books, and came up with ideas' (Goorney 1981: 126). Littlewood's company began this project without a script or playwright, but the group was not completely willing to conclude without an author; according to Robert Leach 'several court cases were fought over the vexed question of authorship' after *Oh What a Lovely War* opened (2006: 160). The printed version of the text has been credited to 'Theatre Workshop, Charles Chilton, and members of the original cast'.

From *Macbeth* to *MacBird!*

No writer in residence was needed for a later satire responding to war. *MacBird!* (1967) was written by Barbara Garson, who shared Littlewood's satiric, anti-war proclivities. The playwright inserted American political machinations and Vietnam War rhetoric into a new version of *Macbeth*. Well received at the Village Gate nightclub in New York, the mock-Elizabethan political intrigue showed President Lyndon 'MacBird' Johnson arranging the assassination of his predecessor, John F. Kennedy. (Johnson's wife was known as Lady Bird long before Garson wrote her play.) As I noted after seeing the New York production, 'the accusation [of JFK's assassination made] against Johnson was preposterous', but 'the substitution of LBJ for Macbeth became a provocative metaphor for the White House as a source of state violence' in Vietnam. 'The primitive weaponry (lance, spiked shoulder pads) and archaic language of a Texan turned Scottish king provide a useful alternative to the veneer of civility and restraint shown in televised press conferences of the sixties, in which the President humbly claimed, "We seek no wider war," while all the time widening the war' (Schechter 1985: 165). Theatre Workshop opened the play in a 'private' Theatre Royal Club after the Lord Chamberlain refused to allow public performances, because *MacBird!* portrayed a friendly state's leader in an unfriendly way. Garson's radical rewriting of Shakespeare first took shape as a skit for an anti-war teach-in at Berkeley, California, where the author had been part of the Free Speech movement. The play seen in England was not exactly the one Garson wrote. According to Nadine Holdsworth, Littlewood turned the performance into 'a vaudeville romp', and critics accused her 'once again, of riding roughshod over an existing text' (2006: 39).

If Littlewood rode roughshod over Garson's satire, adding song and dance, it might have been justified by the fact that Garson rode roughshod over Shakespeare.

MacBird! was not the only American satire shown by Theatre Workshop. In 1961 Theatre Royal, Stratford, presented James Goldman's *They Might Be Giants*. Its comic depiction of a judge who thought he was Sherlock Holmes (a rather British topic) was not so well received. Other satires in the United States stayed there, reaching mainly a counter-cultural audience through the alternative theatres mentioned earlier. In the 1960s stand-up comedians like Mort Sahl, Dick Gregory and Lenny Bruce also addressed political topics in their nightclub acts, as did Nixon impersonators and satiric songwriter Tom Lehrer. New plays that received the most attention in the United States looked at individual and family dysfunction, not crises of national leadership or war. At box-office-conscious commercial and subscriber-based American theatres, the risks of offending patrons and losing income reduced prospects for strong, politically charged satire.

Two inventive full-length satires performed on Broadway since the 1960s, *The Beauty Part* (1962) and *The Producers* (2001), were less concerned with politics than culture. In *The Beauty Part* S. J. Perelman gleefully portrayed the corruption of American artists by commerce. A master of comic language who at one time wrote wisecracks for Marx Brothers films, Perelman placed novelists, publishers, a sculptor, actors and their agents in his play's irreverent parade of sell-outs. In one scene, after an abstract expressionist painter rejects a commission to create a heat-resistant painting on Formica that will hang over a suburban couple's fireplace, he advises would-be artist Lance Weatherwax, a Candide of the culture world: 'Lay off the Muses, buddy, it's is a very tough dollar' (Perelman 1972: 103). The funding and selling out of artists also became a topic for Mel Brooks, who aimed the most effective satire of his play at theatre itself. *The Producers* (discussed earlier) ironically became a highly successful Broadway musical satire about Broadway musicals and their producers.

Laughtivists, Guerrilla Girls and Yes Men

Other writers, directors and theatre groups deserve recognition for their satire, in addition to the three authors whose exemplary plays this survey set out to consider in detail. The theatre form known as satire has a distinguished past that includes far more than the achievements of Aristophanes, Gay, Behan and Littlewood. The future of stage satire is less certain, as artists turn towards other media and locations removed from conventional theatre spaces. Some of the energy, scenic imagination and derisive humour once placed in stage plays can now be found in activist street theatre across England, the United States and in other nations.

Activists from Greenpeace, Reclaim the Streets, Occupy Wall Street, Extinction Rebellion and the Laughtivists have employed satiric scenery, costumes and props for theatrical protests related to war, climate change, wealth inequality, and racial and gender discrimination. Parades, sit-down strikes, urban park occupations, banner hangings and balloon flyovers advance their calls for justice and redress of grievances. Comic slogans, chants and visual displays attract cameras, uplift public spirits, sometimes go viral. The Serbian 'laughtivist' Srdja Popovic combined activism with laughter by throwing a birthday party for Slobodan Milosevic in 1999; birthday gifts for the leader who had been charged with war crimes included a pair of handcuffs, a prison uniform and a one-way ticket to a war crimes tribunal in The Hague. The non-prosecutable party was enjoyed by two thousand of Milosevic's opponents. In 2020 a San Francisco parade of thousands opposing a new war with Iran featured a lookalike of the President of the United States wearing a suit of black-and-white prison stripes; the nation's leader had seemingly come out of jail to support anti-war protesters. Not quite the same imagery took flight when a giant hot-air balloon representing 'Baby Donald Trump' floated over London to cast a comic shadow on the temper-tantrum-prone President's visit in 2019. 'Baby Trump' flying past Parliament could be seen internationally in press photos, and copies of him soon began taking to the air in the United States. The balloons, along with giant puppets, banners, festively dressed marchers chanting 'This is what democracy looks like', create participatory, enthusiastic communities analogous to those applauding a satiric stage performance; only they are not seated or watching a play.

The festivity of satire on stage can initiate experiences of solidarity and engagement that protest marches and rallies offer participants; and vice versa. Both forms of assembly let a large body act (or support actors) in the name of particular social needs and political concerns. Future stage satire parallel to, and in concert with, political dissent and community assemblies, presented in playhouses, tours and one-person shows, has exemplary precedents mentioned in Chapters 1 to 3.

One feminist group that sustained its satire outside conventional theatres for decades, The Guerrilla Girls, formed in 1985. Members still wear gorilla masks and fake fur, and anonymously criticize art galleries for their discrimination against female artists and artists of colour. Identities hidden behind their masks, the Guerrilla Girls have thrown bananas to spectators who asked a provocative question at their public discussions of art. Some of them can be booked in advance for a public appearance. Their satiric posters (now collector's items) pasted outside art galleries and museums humorously describe the bias of exhibits. Masked participants in GG actions are rumoured to include prominent artists such as Jenny Holzer and Cindy Sherman, but names used in their statements are often those of women no longer available for public questioning: Frida Kahlo, Bertha Morisot, and others valued less than male counterparts when they were alive.

The Yes Men, a group started in 1999 and still in business, devise public interventions comparable to those of the Guerrilla Girls; only these disguised activists claim to be corporate executives. They perform at specially arranged press conferences and through electronic mail. Impersonating

CEOs, the men announce new, beneficial programs on behalf of their alleged companies. They awarded a pardon to exiled whistleblower Edward Snowden, promised payment for environmental damages done by a large energy supplier, planned for a Swiss manufacturer to convert from armaments to windmill production. The Yes Men announce corporate reforms that they would like to see. Reporters mistake them for highly paid executives. One of the group's founders, Andy Bichlbaum, called their art 'identity correction' and advised those who would practice it to 'find a target – some entity running amok – and think of something true they could say but never would – something that's also lots of fun' (2012: 60). The art of satiric impersonation pioneered by Jonathan Swift when he created the persona of M. B. Drapier to mock British monetary policy has returned with new, computer-literate performers who appear in person (disguised) and extend their reach online through widely distributed press releases.

Despite their live meetings with the public, the Guerrilla Girls and the Yes Men are known primarily through their publications, websites and the media coverage of their satire. Their dependence on digitalized documentation is not entirely different from that of satirist Michael Moore, best known for his quasi-documentary films. Cameras recorded his personal encounters with questionable corporate authorities and distressed citizens in *Roger and Me, Fahrenheit 911, Sicko* and *Bowling for Columbine*.

Armando Iannucci's recent films and television programs also ridicule highly placed officials; but while Moore pursues the actual officials, Iannucci has actors portray them. His film *The Death of Stalin* reconstructed grotesque Kremlin infighting among Stalin's successors. *Veep* imagined a female Vice-President of the United States struggling to be noticed in the shadow of the White House. Iannucci's satires tend to look at inept, cowardly and misinformed politicians and their aides in comedy reminiscent of the earlier popular British television program *Yes, Minister*. Moore's political satire is more personal, as he pursues Very Important People to question them and promote universal healthcare, lead-free drinking water and gun control. Through films, mass media coverage and websites the Yes Men, the Guerrilla Girls, Iannucci and Moore have reached a widely dispersed and varied audience. One drawback to their advances is that they do not bring spectators and actors together to interact in large groups as stage satire did in the past. Rallies and marches do this to some extent; but the diminution of the 'commons' – in this case, the loss of shared theatre space where actors, satirists and spectators can see and hear one another in person repeatedly, the loss of that community for satire – marks the beginning of the end for a theatre form.

5

Conclusion: The Endangered Future of Satire

The experience that satire on stage offered audiences in ancient Athens, eighteenth-century London and mid-twentieth-century Stratford has few equivalents today. Aristophanes, Gay and Behan are still performed on occasion; but their topical playwriting is not likely to be as current, humorous and provocative as it was – more of a tribute to theatre's distinguished past. Satire still can be seen on the street and online; but these locations do not serve the 'commons' and its assembly of laughter, with spectator involvement in extended comic recognition scenes and interactions with actors as satiric plays have in the past.

Satire fares better on film and television in some respects. It can be watched any time a recording is available. Stanley Kubrick's *Dr. Strangelove, or How I Learned to Stop Worrying and Love the Bomb* (1964), with its mockery of nuclear war planners in the 1960s, remains a laudably directed comic nightmare. Actor Peter Sellers, portraying Dr Strangelove, is as manic as ever. New audiences seeing his mad scientist today may not connect Strangelove to the men who inspired his character, ex-Nazi scientist Werner von Braun and nuclear war theorist Herman Kahn. Viewers also might not know that the Pentagon's mid-twentieth-century strategy of MAD (mutual assured destruction) was not a joke but an acronym for a serious plan to deter nuclear war through threats of total annihilation. The final image in Kubrick's film, where one crazy, determined American soldier waves his ten-gallon cowboy hat and flies to an enemy target on the back of a bomb that will set off the Doomsday Machine and destroy the world, stands as a tribute to Hollywood westerns as well as MAD planners. Still, for all *Dr. Strangelove's* apocalyptic humour, the satire is no longer so timely; newer, less personal systems of bomb delivery, hypersonic and drone-flown death threats, require a different vision of the world's end.

Live theatrical satire is more sustainable and renewable; when a play is restaged, if its topical references and actor impersonations are adeptly revised within an existing dramatic structure, the performance can surprise and delight. This was shown when Brecht adapted *The Beggar's Opera*, and Fo adapted biblical lore for *Mistero Buffo*. Despite stage satire's renewal by these artists and others, the form's capacity to ridicule illicit behaviour in public and unite an audience of hundreds or thousands through laughter has become an endangered asset, as audiences stay home to watch cable TV or programs streaming online. The situation was exacerbated in 2020 when a pandemic virus closed theatres, museums and libraries; people practiced 'social distance', physically staying away from one another and from live performances. Challenges that home viewing and digitization had already posed to the cultural commons increased.

While far less harmful than a pandemic, electronically broadcast entertainments have not only kept people at home, but also reduced the ability of artists to control their work's content, as network executives, commercial sponsors and corporate regulations place limits on free expression. Stage satire in its most basic form requires only a few actors and spectators, no expensive equipment or wealthy sponsors. When Dario Fo and Franca Rame found their satire censored on a popular national television program, *Canzonissima*, they left the airwaves and toured their own shows. The large, attentive following they initially secured on Italian TV was eager to see them in person during the stage tours that began in 1967. (A later ban placed on them by the US State Department only made their work more popular when they arrived in America.)

Fo and Rame raised funds from ticket sales, but free public satire supported by subsidies should not be ruled out in the future. A few wealthy patrons following the example of the *choregoi* (producers) in ancient Athens might be persuaded to pay for a Theatre of Satire and end the need for admission fees. A new Federal Theatre Project in the United States or a decent British Arts Council grant could encourage such theatre too. Whether any political or civic leaders will agree to fund these programs, and not withdraw support if offended, is another question. Could elected officials or wealthy benefactors be persuaded that historically satire has been as important to democracy as the Assembly in Athens, more beneficial to the public (to invoke Swift's comment on Gay's ballad opera) than a thousand sermons? Could a Theatre of Satire become a resource valued as highly as the multiple military bands America's Pentagon generously funds, and receive equally generous government support for its humorous attacks? Only a satirist or a theatre historian would ask such questions.

Augusto Boal's Mayor, John Gay's Puppeteers

Another model for future satire was advanced by Augusto Boal, the Brazilian director and creator of Theatre of the Oppressed. I heard him describe a town where residents were unable to speak with their mayor; the official refused to talk with them in a public forum. Constituents announced that a stand-in, a community member, would impersonate the mayor and take their questions. When he heard the plan to replace him, his

Honour appeared at the forum himself, ready to talk. Though not so humorous in its final phase, the event was a variant on the art of satiric impersonation. Boal himself was elected as *vereador* (legislator) in Rio de Janeiro in 1992, and turned his office into a theatre project. He invited constituents to become 'legislative actors' and devise laws he then submitted for passage by other elected officials (Boal 1998: 16–18).

Civic leaders also confronted a theatre group and inadvertently advanced its satire of them in John Gay's eighteenth-century play, *The Rehearsal at Goatham*, discussed earlier but deserving further mention. The plot of the play draws on Gay's personal experience of censorship under Walpole. In Goatham puppeteers find their show has been cancelled. Offering a reason for the decision made by town leaders, a character named Oaf contends that Peter and his 'puppetshew' will 'turn the whole corporation of Goatham into ridicule'. His companion Gosling adds: 'Nothing alive but puppets would dare to be so insolent; for we see all well-bred men now-a-days pay the due homage to riches and power as they ought' (Gay 1760: 368–9). Neither of these objectors have seen or read the puppet play they condemn. Out of a negative vision of satire and its anticipated threat to those with 'riches and power', as well as his own past experience, Gay created this new satire. He was not the only one who looked back to move forward; authors who adapted Gay's *The Beggar's Opera* were following his example, whether or not they knew it. Satire of the future was discovered in the past as well as the present, through a process Brecht termed reutilization (*Umfunktionierung*) (Mayer 1971: 89).

Brecht's observations about satire in the 1930s also apply to the form's future. Referring to Jonathan Swift's 'fire and thoroughness' in the 'modest proposal' to market poor people's infants as edibles, Brecht thought (as noted earlier) that the Irish pamphleteer's ironic 'nastiness would be fully recognizable to anyone', and saw a need for more of such 'base' thinking in response to Hitler's reign. Under the Nazis, when the 'starving are cursed as greedy, those who have nothing to defend [are cursed] as cowards, those who doubt their oppressor [cursed] as those who doubt their own strength', 'thinking in general counts as base and falls into disrepute'. Swift's kind of 'base' thinking was needed to defend the hungry and the oppressed in the 1930s (Brecht 2003: 152–3). The need has not abated, as inequality, warfare and threats to democratic decision-making continue, worsened by climate emergencies, technologically advanced militarism, post-Nazi white nationalism. Topics suitable for satire will not be in short supply in the future, although venues for public performance and stage artists engaged in the form may be harder to find.

In earlier discussion, the rise of electronic media was said to abet stage satire's decline; it may be more accurate to say that new media have reduced the need for writing satire, as technology enables government leaders and celebrities to look foolish on their own. Their ridiculous behaviour can be recorded and quickly replayed. Televised satirists such as Jon Stuart and Trevor Noah on *The Daily Show* 'quote' events through film clips and Twitter transcriptions. The electronic images and recorded words of a politician or celebrity, removed from their imposing setting and re-framed by comic commentary, are exposed as meretricious, vain and nonsensical. Taking quotations from press conferences, public speeches and interviews, the scenes replayed adeptly expose what Benjamin termed 'the empty phrase', its vacuity more evident when quoted by a satirist (1999: 435). There is work for a satirist here, as he or she can introduce the quoted material; but cameramen, film editors and broadcasters are needed more than a playwright or group of actors for these presentations.

One example of this technologically advanced satire was broadcast on 3 April 2020 on *The Daily Show*. Trevor Noah introduced a brief, ironic 'Salute to the Heroes of the Coronavirus Pandemic'. Film clips from preceding weeks quoted conservative pundits and Donald Trump dismissing the not yet arrived Covid-19 virus as no more dangerous than the flu or a common cold. Aired at a time when a pandemic was killing tens of thousands and threatening millions worldwide, the film sequence made the so-called 'heroes' look ill-informed, unfit to lead with the kind of misinformation they shared. The last filmed quotation in the series showed the President of the United States, after weeks of denying any danger, claiming he knew all along a pandemic was coming. (He just neglected to tell the public.) No playwright or actor was needed to portray this folly, although Trevor Noah's amused look made his reaction visible. As Karl Kraus said in his preface to *The Last Days of Mankind*: 'the most improbable conversations here were spoken word for word, the more lurid fantasies are quotations' (Kraus 2015: 1). Kraus's satiric approach to a crisis remains quite practicable.

Instead of a Conclusion, Continuation

Rather than end by predicting further decline in the performance of stage satire, I want to propose a number of programs to keep this form of theatre alive.

(1) **Live performance that begins with film, television and the internet.** Some sites online already display verbal and visual satire. These sources along with newscasts and film clips could serve as cues for live satire, a kind of reversal of recording, with actors in front of a theatre audience inspired by and responding to electronic recordings. Actors might offer a live re-enactment of a recent event at the White House, Downing Street or the Kremlin; but add to it, imagine an alternative. As Dario Fo observed: 'Power bends over backwards to ensure that people's native imagination atrophies, that they eschew the effort involved in developing alternative ideas on what is occurring around them from those purveyed by the mass media' (Fo 1991: 118). A satirist on stage responding to a filmed press conference also could

take a cue from Brecht's 1934 essay, 'On Restoring the Truth', and 'slowly, but utterly, he corrects what he has heard... he places correct sentences alongside incorrect ones... When he hears that wars are necessary, then he adds under which circumstances they are necessary, as well as: for whom' (2003: 133). The respondent would add humour, too, if it is not already there.

(2) **Festivals and workshops** for revival and reutilization of past satires: classic satires can be staged anew, with the plays revised where needed, to inspire, instruct and entertain. Ancient Athenian satire thrived in festivals, so might new works based on the old. If the festivals cannot be state-sponsored, university theatres and free public workshops subsidized by artists and their well-wishers offer the best settings for these projects. Participants can learn the art of satire from open rehearsals, staged readings, improvised new scenes, and collaboration with professional ensembles.

(3) **Street theatre and interventions in everyday life** require only a few actors and spectators. Satires could be performed outdoors, unannounced in marketplaces, parks and transit centres, on small portable stages in front of the offices of elected officials and courthouses. Fo and Rame used to perform trial scenes outside courthouses for the public that couldn't gain admission to a trial inside. Humorous visuals could be introduced in parade floats, puppet shows, antic marching bands and large, colourful banners. Mass media and social media might take notice of these offerings, and amplify their impact. Boal's writing in *Theatre of the Oppressed* offers more ideas for such events, as do Welfare State's book *Engineers of the Imagination* and Fo's *The Tricks of the Trade*.

(4) **A new play not yet written** could begin with the following scenario, suitable for an improvisation or completion, with apologies to Boal, Fo, Gay

and other sources of inspiration. The scenario: The leading politician of a certain country objects to an announced plan for impersonation of him in a stage play. He has not seen the play: it is still being written; but he declares that he will not go to see it, and none of his followers should either. It couldn't possibly be entertaining, and never as entertaining as he is. He threatens to put on his own show, but admits he has no time to rehearse, hates theatre, has an election campaign to win, new Draconian laws to impose and administer, golf greens await him also. Thanks to this publicity, demand for tickets to the new satire is unceasing; the play is sold out months ahead of its first preview. The playwright wonders whether it would be better to keep working on the project indefinitely as rumours about its controversial scenes increase. Critics begin to analyse the work before seeing it. Actors audition in public, performing imagined speeches at a time no auditions are being held. The politician defends himself against the stage portrayal that has never been seen, and in doing so he turns into the figure he fears people will see. He offers a bad imitation of himself. The author decides there is no need for his play, and instead runs for office.

(5) **Karl Kraus explains the satirist's need to continue his art,** in advice written after Hitler took power in 1933: 'For as long as someone rings a bell with [the satirist], so long as some swindler provides an appropriate model, he must be concerned not to lose them, and no one can imagine the unending trepidation that satirists have on that score' (Kraus 2020: 14).

(6) **The consolations of history** can be found reading satiric texts and accounts of their performance. While waiting for a new Aristophanes, another Fo and Rame, or a successor to Joan Littlewood and her workshop, we can celebrate past stage satirists and their accomplishments, wish they were here.

FURTHER READING/ BIBLIOGRAPHY

Abrams, M.A. (1985), *A Glossary of Literary Terms*, Fort Worth: Holt, Reinhart and Winston.

Aristophanes (1969), *Four Comedies (Lysistrata, The Acharnians, The Congresswomen, The Frogs)*, edited by William Arrowsmith, Ann Arbor: University of Michigan Press.

Aristophanes (1979), *Clouds, Women in Power, Knights*, translated by Kenneth McLeish, Cambridge: Cambridge University Press.

Aristophanes (1986), *The Knights, Peace, The Birds, The Assemblywomen, Wealth*, translated by Alan Sommerstein and David Barrett, New York: Penguin Books.

Aristophanes (1993), *Plays One* (including *Peace, Knights, Acharnians, Lysistrata*), translated by Kenneth McLeish, London: Methuen.

Aristophanes (1996), *Three Plays (Lysistrata, Women at the Thesmophoria, Assemblywomen)*, translated by Jeffrey Henderson, London: Routledge.

Aristophanes (1998), *Acharnians, Knights*, translated by Jeffrey Henderson, Cambridge: Harvard University Press.

Aristotle (1961), *The Poetics*, translated by S.H. Butcher, New York: Hill and Wang.

Behan, Brendan (1959), *The Hostage*, New York: Grove Press.

Behan, Brendan (1962a), *The Hostage*, London: Methuen.

Behan, Brendan (1962b), *Brendan Behan's Island: An Irish Sketchbook* with drawings by Paul Hogarth, London: Hutchinson.

Behan, Brendan (1963), *Hold Your Hour and Have Another*, Boston: Little, Brown and Company.

Behan, Brendan (1978), *The Complete Plays*, introduced by Alan Simpson, New York: Grove Press.

Behan, Brendan (1987), *An Giall* [Gaelic text of *The Hostage*], translated and edited by Richard Wall, and *The Hostage*, edited by Richard Wall, Washington, DC: Catholic University of America Press.

Benjamin, Walter (1977), *Understanding Brecht*, London: New Left Books.

Benjamin, Walter (1999), 'Karl Kraus', in *Selected Writings, Volume 2*, edited by Michael W. Jennings, Howard Eiland and Gary Smith, translated by Rodney Livingston and others, Cambridge: Belknap Press.

Bharucha, Rustom (1979), 'Politics and Satire in India: The Theater of Utpal Dutt', *Theater*, 10, no. 2.

Bichlbaum, Andy (2012), 'Identity Correction', in *Beautiful Trouble*, edited by Andrew Boyd and Dave Mitchell, New York: OR Books.

Boal, Augusto (1998), *Legislative Theatre*, London: Routledge.

Boswell, Samuel (1923), *The Life of Samuel Johnson*, London: J.M. Dent and Sons.

Braun, Edward, ed. and trans. (1969), *Meyerhold on Theatre*, New York: Hill and Wang.

Brecht, Bertolt (1957), *Brecht on Theatre*, translated by John Willett, New York: Hill and Wang.

Brecht, Bertolt (1976), *The Resistible Rise of Arturo Ui*, translated by Ralph Manheim, in *Collected Plays, Volume 6*, edited by Ralph Manheim and John Willett. New York: Random House.

Brecht, Bertolt (1979), *The Threepenny Opera*, translated by Ralph Manheim and John Willett, London: Methuen.

Brecht, Bertolt (1994), *Collected Plays, Volume 7 (Visions of Simone Machard, Schweyk in the Second World War, Caucasian Chalk Circle, The Duchess of Malfi)*, edited by John Willett and Ralph Manheim, London: Methuen Drama.

Brecht, Bertolt (2003), *Brecht on Art and Politics*, edited by Tom Kuhn and Steve Giles, London: Methuen Drama.

Brecht, Bertolt (2019), *The Collected Poems of Bertolt Brecht*, translated and edited by Tom Kuhn and David Constantine, New York: Liveright.

Brecht, Bertolt (2020), *Refugee Conversations*, translated by Romy Fursland, edited and introduced by Tom Kuhn, London: Methuen Drama.

Brien, Alan (1982), 'Brendan Behan: "Uproarious Tragedy"', in *Brendan Behan: Interviews and Recollections*, Volume 2, edited by E.H. Mikhail, Totowar, NJ: Barnes and Noble Books.

Brooks, Mel and Meehan, Tom (2001), *The Producers*, New York: Hyperion.

Brustein, Robert (1965), *Seasons of Discontent*, New York: Simon and Schuster.

Bulgakov, Mikhail (1986), *The Life of Monsieur de Molière*, translated by Mirra Ginsberg, New York: New Directions.

Bulgakov, Mikhail (1991), *Six Plays*, translated by Michael Glenny and William Powell, London: Methuen Drama.

Case, Sue-Ellen (1988), *Feminism and Theatre*, London: Methuen.

Cave, Richard, Schafer, Elizabeth and Woolland, Brian, eds (1979), *Ben Jonson and Theatre*, London: Routledge.

Chambers, David (1998), 'The Master of Praxis [Meyerhold]', *Theater*, 28, no. 2.

Churchill, Caryl (1985), *Plays: One*, New York: Routledge.

Collins-Hughes, Laura (2020), 'The Fourth Wall Is My Laptop', *New York Times*, 27 March.

Deerwester, Jayme (2019), 'Trump Tweets: "Should Federal Election Commission and/or FCC Look into "SNL?"'' *USA Today*, 18 March, online.

Ehrenberg, Victor (1962), *The People of Aristophanes: A Sociology of Old Attic Comedy*, New York: Schocken Books.

Elliott, Robert C. (1960), *The Power of Satire: Magic, Ritual, Art*, Princeton: Princeton University Press.

Empson, William (1975), '*The Beggar's Opera*: Mock Pastoral as the Cult of Independence', in *Twentieth Century Interpretations of the Beggar's Opera*, edited by Yvonne Noble, Englewood Cliffs, NJ: Prentice Hall, Inc.

Erdman, Nicholai (1979), *The Suicide*, translated by Peter Tegel, London: Pluto Press.

Erdman, Nicholai (1995), *A Meeting about Laughter: Sketches, Interludes, and Theatrical Parodies,* translated and edited by John Freedman, Luxembourg: Harwood Academic Publishers GmbH.

Fiske, Roger (1975), 'English Theatre Music in the Eighteenth Century', in *Twentieth Century Interpretations of the Beggar's Opera*, edited by Yvonne Noble, Englewood Cliffs, NJ: Prentice Hall, Inc.

Fo, Dario (1980), *Accidental Death of an Anarchist*, adapted by Gavin Richards, with an introduction by Dario Fo, London: Pluto Press.

Fo, Dario (1983), *About Face*, translated by Dale McAddo and Charles Mann, *Theater*, 14, no. 3.

Fo, Dario (1984), *Trumpets and Raspberries*, translated by R.C. McAvoy and A.M. Giugni, London: Pluto Press.

Fo, Dario (1988), 'The Birth of the Jongleurs', in *Mistero Buffo*, translated by Ed Emery, London: Methuen.

Fo, Dario (1991), *The Tricks of the Trade*, translated by Joe Farrell, New York: Routledge.

Foucault, Michel (1977), 'What Is an Author?' in *Language, Counter-Memory, Practice*, edited by Donald F. Bouchard, Ithaca: Cornell University.

Garson, Barbara (1967), *MacBird!*, New York: Grove Press.

Gassner, John, ed. (1963), *Medieval and Tudor Drama*, New York: Bantam Drama.

Gay, John (1760), *Plays*, London: J & R Tonson.

Gay, John (1969), '*The What D'Ye Call It*', in *Burlesque Plays of the Eighteenth Century*, edited by Simon Trussler, London: Oxford University Press.

Gay, John (1973), *The Beggar's Opera*, with an introduction by Oswald Doughty, New York: Dover.

Gay, John (2013), *The Beggar's Opera* and *Polly*, edited with an introduction by Hal Gladfelder, Oxford: Oxford University Press.

Goorney, Howard (1981), *The Theatre Workshop Story*, London: Eyre Methuen.

Guerinot, J.V. and Jilg, Rodney (1976), *Contexts 1: The Beggar's Opera*, Hamden, CT: Archon Books.

Halliwell, Stephen (1984), 'Aristophanic Satire', in *English Satire and the Satiric Tradition*, edited by Claude Rawson, Oxford: Basil Blackwell.

Herondas (1981), *The Mimes of Herondas*, translated by Guy Davenport, San Francisco: Grey Fox Press.

Highet, Gilbert (1962), *An Anatomy of Satire*, Princeton: Princeton University Press.

Holdsworth, Nadine (2006), *Joan Littlewood*, London: Routledge.

Juvenal (1958), *The Satires of Juvenal*, translated by Rolfe Humphries, Bloomington: Indiana University Press.

Kernan, Alvin (1965), *The Plot of Satire*, New Haven: Yale University Press.

Kershaw, Baz (1992), *The Politics of Performance: Radical Theatre as Cultural Intervention*, London: Routledge.

Kott, Jan (1968), *Theatre Notebook*, New York: Doubleday.

Kraus, Karl (2015), *The Last Days of Mankind*, translated by Fred Bridgham and Edward Timms, New Haven: Yale University Press.

Kraus, Karl (2020), *The Third Walpurgis Night*, translated by Fred Bridgeham and Edward Timms, New Haven: Yale University Press.

Kurtz, Eric (1975), 'The Shepherd as Gamester: Musical Mock-Pastoral in *The Beggar's Opera*', in *Twentieth Century Interpretations of the Beggar's Opera*, edited by Yvonne Noble, Englewood Cliffs, NJ: Prentice Hall, Inc.

Leach, Robert (2006), *Theatre Workshop: Joan Littlewood and the Making of Modern British Theatre*, Exeter: University of Exeter Press.

Littlewood, Joan (1965), 'Goodbye Note from Joan', in *The Encore Reader*, edited by Charles Marowitz, Tom Milne and Owen Hale, London: Methuen.

Littlewood, Joan (1994), *Joan's Book: Joan Littlewood's Peculiar History as She Tells It*, London: Methuen.

MacCraith, Micheal (2019), 'Brendan Behan and Elie Wiesel: *An Giall* and *L'Aube*', in *Reading Brendan Behan*, edited by John McCourt, Cork: Cork University Press.

MacDowell, Douglas (1995), *Aristophanes and Athens*, Oxford: Oxford University Press.

McGrath, John (1981), *A Good Night Out*, London: Eyre Methuen.

McMahon, Deirdre (2019), 'Brendan Behan: Modernist Writer', in *Reading Brendan Behan*, edited by John McCourt, Cork: Cork University Press.

Marowitz, Charles (1965), 'Littlewood Pays a Dividend', in *The Encore Reader*, edited by Charles Marowitz, Tom Milne and Owen Hale, London: Methuen.

Marx, Karl (1963), *The Eighteenth Brumaire of Louis Bonaparte*, New York: International Publishers.

Mayakovsky, Vladimir (1968), *The Complete Plays of Vladimir Mayakovsky*, translated by Guy Daniels, New York: Simon and Schuster.

Mayer, Hans (1971), 'Bertolt Brecht and the Tradition', in *Steppenwolf and Everyman*, translated by Jack Zipes, New York: Thomas Y. Crowell Company.

Milligan, Spike and Antrobus, John (1979), *The Bedsitting Room*, London: W.H. Allen & Co.

Molière, Jean Baptiste Poquelin (1982), *The Misanthrope* and *Tartuffe*, translated by Richard Wilbur, New York: Harcourt, Inc.

Montoya, Richard, Salinas, Ricardo and Siguenza, Herbert (1998), *Culture Clash: Life Death and Revolutionary Comedy*, New York: Theatre Communications Group.

Nadir, Moyshe (2018), *Messiah in America*, translated by Michael Shapiro, Rennes: Farlag Press.

Ni Riordain, Cliona (2019), 'Brendan Behan's *The Hostage*: Translation, Adaptation or Recreation of An Giall?' in *Reading Brendan Behan*, edited by John McCourt, Cork: Cork University Press.

Norman, Larry F. (2006), 'Molière as Satirist', in *The Cambridge Companion to Moliere*, edited by David Bradby and Andrew Calder, Cambridge: Cambridge University Press.

Ono, Yoko (1964), *Grapefruit*, New York: Simon & Schuster.

Orwell, George (1953), *A Collection of Essays*, New York: Harcourt, Brace Jovanovich, Inc.

Perelman, S.J. (1972), 'The Beauty Part', in *Broadway's Beautiful Losers*, edited by Marilyn Stasio, New York: Delta.

Quintana, Ricardo (1964), 'Situational Satire: A Commentary on the Method of Swift', in *Swift*, edited by Ernest Tuveson, Englewood Cliffs, NJ: Prentice-Hall, Inc.

Romma, James (2016), 'Culture Desk: Trump Versus Clinton', *The New Yorker*, 13 October. www.newyorker.com/culture/culture-desk/trump-versus-clinton.

Russo, Carlo Fernando (1994), *Aristophanes: An Author for the Stage*, London: Routledge.

Schafer, Elizabeth (1999), 'Daughters of Ben', in *Ben Jonson and Theatre*, edited by Richard Cave, Elizabeth Schafer and Brian Woolland, London: Routledge, 154–78.

Schechter, Joel (1985), *Durov's Pig: Clowns, Politics and Theatre*, New York: Theatre Communications Group.

Schechter, Joel (1994), *Satiric Impersonations: From Aristophanes to the Guerrilla Girls*, Carbondale, IL: Southern Illinois University Press.

Schechter, Joel (2008), *Messiahs of 1933: How American Yiddish Theatre Survived Adversity through Satire*, Philadelphia: Temple University Press.

Schechter, Joel (2016), *Eighteenth-Century Brechtians: Theatrical Satire in the Age of Walpole*, Exeter: University of Exeter Press.

Segal, Erich, ed. (1996), *Oxford Readings in Aristophanes*, Oxford: Oxford University Press.

Senelick, Laurence (1993), *Cabaret Performance, Volume II, Europe 1920–1940*, Baltimore: Johns Hopkins University Press.

Shakespeare, William (1960), *Works*, New York: Oxford University Press (Shakespeare Head Press reprint).

Silk, M.S. (2000), *Aristophanes and the Definition of Comedy*, New York: Oxford University Press.

Smeliansky, Anatoly (1990), 'A Play That Will Not Be Closed: Nikolai Erdman's "Suicide" at Taganka Theatre', *Moscow News Weekly*, no. 32, p. 14.

Smeliansky, Anatoly (1993), *Is Comrade Bulgakov Dead?: Mikhail Bulgakov at the Moscow Art Theatre*, New York: Routledge.

Solonos, Alexis (1974), *The Living Aristophanes*, Ann Arbor: University of Michigan Press.

Soyinka, Wole (1981), *Opera Wonyosi*, Bloomington: Indiana University Press.

Spalter, Max (1967), *Brecht's Tradition*, Baltimore: Johns Hopkins Press.

Swann, Caroline (1982), 'There's No Place on Earth Like the World', in *Brendan Behan: Interviews and Recollections*, Volume 2, edited by E.H. Mikhail, Totowar, NJ: Barnes and Noble Books.

Swift, Jonathan (1704), *A Tale of a Tub and A Battel Between the Books Antient and Modern*, London: John Nutt.

Swift, Jonathan (1730), 'A Vindication of Mr. Gay, and *The Beggar's Opera*', in *The Intelligencer*, London: Francis Cogan.

Swift, Jonathan (1754), 'Mad Mullinix and Timothy' and 'The Journal of a Modern Lady', in *The Works of Dr. Jonathan Swift*, Volume 6, London: C. Bathhurst.

Swift, Jonathan (1801), '"Letter to Thomas Sheridan" (1718 poem) in "Works, Volume 7"', *Wikisource online*.

Theatre Workshop, Charles Chilton, and members of the original cast (1965), *Oh What a Lovely War*, London: Methuen.

Thomas, June (2006), 'Joan Littlewood's Revelations', *Slate*, 10 May, online.

Thucydides (1972), *History of the Peloponnesian War*, translated by Rex Warner, London: Penguin Classics.

Tynan, Kenneth (1961), *Curtains*, New York: Atheneum.

Willett, John (1968), *The Theatre of Bertolt Brecht*, New York: New Directions.

Williams, Raymond (1979), *Modern Tragedy*, London: Verso.

Worthington, Ian (1987), 'Aristophanes' Knights and the Abortive Peace Proposals of 425 B.C.', *L'Antiquite Classique*, 56, pp. 56–7.

INDEX